The
A.J. Meerwald
and NEW JERSEY'S OYSTER INDUSTRY

Constance McCart, EdD
& Rachel Rodgers Dolhanczyk, MA

THE
History
PRESS

Published by The History Press
Charleston, SC
www.historypress.com

Front cover, bottom: The schooner *A.J. Meerwald* as seen from the barquentine *Gazela. Bayshore Collection, gift of the photographer Captain Mitch Brodkin, 2007.*

First published 2021

ISBN 9781540250452

Library of Congress Control Number: 2021945853

CONTENTS

Contents

FOREWORD

*O*ur country's history is deeply intertwined with the maritime trades; from Melville to Twain, the necessity of a waterborne economy has left an indelible imprint on our culture. Today, only a few relics of the grand ships and small working craft that built this country remain. As a professional shipwright, I have had many opportunities to build, restore and maintain vessels of historic significance in my home state of Maine and beyond. My work has also allowed me to participate in the operation of many historic and traditional vessels in both commercial and educational capacities, even serving as ship's carpenter on a square-rigged sail-training ship touring the Atlantic Ocean. My travels have shown me how education focused on maritime history, seamanship, craftsmanship and the environment enriches people's lives.

The value of these experiences cannot be overstated. In an ideal world, every state with navigable waters would have at least one vessel that serves as an ambassador of the region's maritime heritage and a platform for education, but unfortunately, this is not the case. The state of New Jersey is extremely fortunate to be one of the few that possesses one such vessel, and one that is indeed a national treasure of historic importance. The schooner *A.J. Meerwald* exists today thanks to dedicated visionaries who saw value in the bones of a tired old hulk, well past a state of usefulness, as a tool for commerce and nearing the end of its life. With great skill and careful planning, the last vestiges of Delaware Bay's wooden shipbuilding past were revived, and in the mid-1990s, *A.J. Meerwald* was given new life to carry her into the future with a mission that is arguably her most important occupation yet.

My business partner Garett Eisele and I began working with Bayshore Center at Bivalve in 2018, when we were asked to assess the current condition of the schooner for future maintenance planning. Since that time, we have become well acquainted with *A.J. Meerwald* and have done several small repairs where the vessel resides on the Maurice River. During our visits to Bivalve, Garett and I learned much about the rich history and economic significance of the Delaware Bay oyster industry, as well as the beauty and ecological importance of the bay and its tributaries.

In the pages that follow, Connie McCart and Rachel Dolhanczyk will survey the storied history of southern New Jersey's oyster dredging past and the prosperous era that inspired Delaware Bay watermen to perfect the practice of dredging under sail before thousands of years of sailing evolution were abandoned in favor of internal combustion engines. Dr. McCart and Ms. Dolhanczyk delve into the origins of the *A.J. Meerwald* and what led to the eventual restoration after decades of transformation and deterioration. This historical context allows us to understand *A.J. Meerwald's* critical role in educating New Jersey's youth about the history and ecology of their surroundings—education that is even more urgent in the face of environmental changes and the impending collapse of our fisheries.

As I write, my company is preparing for a planned second restoration of the *Meerwald*, which will include a new deck and deck-level components. A quarter century of service and thousands of passengers and students treading the *Meerwald's* deck have necessitated substantial repair work to keep the vessel healthy and sound for future generations. It is an absolute honor to be a part of this continued story and to help ensure that the schooner keeps sailing for years to come. The shipwrights and schooner captains of Cumberland County are long gone today, but their legacy lives on in "New Jersey's Tallship," the schooner *A.J. Meerwald.*

—Tim Clark
Clark & Eisele Traditional Boatbuilding, Lincolnville, Maine

INTRODUCTION

*I*t is a warm, late spring day in Bivalve. The schooner makes her way down the Maurice River toward the bay with all three sails deployed and full from the wind. It has been over an hour since we left the dock, and we've helped hoist the sails, deployed the trawl net and explored the deck.

A crew member reminds the students and passengers on board that this is "quiet time" and they should be listening to the natural sounds around them and observing the water and nearby land. We settle down in the sun to listen: the sound of the heavy canvas sails snapping in the breeze; a few calls from the seagulls going by; the ship creaking slightly as she moves through the water. We can smell the briny water, the odoriferous clam factory operating nearby, the fish and crabs brought in on the trawl.

The captain interrupts to call attention to the sky—overhead, a majestic bald eagle flies over, headed toward a nest in the meadow where a number of pairs have taken up residence. Cameras and phones click as everyone murmurs appreciatively. This moment alone would have been worth the day's trip.

—Connie McCart

> *Dear Bayshore Center, My favorite things [were] all of them. But the best was when the fish was on my face. It felt slimy and weird. Thank you for doing this. From Leonardo*

The *A.J. Meerwald* under sail. *Bayshore Collection.*

> *Dear Bayshore Center, I loved this field trip. You guys did an amazing job. One of my favorite things was the migration butterfly when we got to play but also learn. Another one of my favorite things is when we got to go on the boat and put up the sail and learn about the [oysters]. Your Friend Keyla*

The schooner the *A.J. Meerwald* has more than earned her place in New Jersey's history. Locally built in 1928, the gaff-rigged oyster schooner was commissioned by the Meerwald family as part of the then-thriving New Jersey oyster industry located on the Delaware Bay. This corner of Cumberland County, now one of the poorest in New Jersey, was once the home of millionaires and of towns that are now either just remnants of their former selves or gone altogether. Tracing the early life of the boat also traces the rise of that industry over a span of decades within the industrial age, fed by the easy access of railroads, the invention of the refrigerated rail car and the relative affordability of the oyster.

As happens, circumstances changed. A depression, a world war, a labor shortage, methods of dredging that harmed the ecosystem and, finally, the appearance of major diseases among the oysters would put the business into a tailspin, while the *Meerwald* was lost to bankruptcy and found herself without sails and reinvented working elsewhere and, in the end, resting unhappily on a riverbank.

But rescue came, and the *A.J. Meerwald* would eventually be restored to begin a new life as an icon of New Jersey. Many volunteer hours and grant contributions were invested in not only the ship but also her environment. The wharf, once crowded with schooners, would now be hers alone, and the shipping sheds, once restored, house the Bayshore Center, the *Meerwald's* owner and operator. She presently tours the shores of New Jersey, offering public sails and school excursions from Trenton to Cape May to Alpine with a devoted following and repeat customer sailings of over 60 percent. Shore-based initiatives abound, and the Bivalve shipping sheds have become a community gathering place, a cultural center and a strong advocate for the ecology of the area.

This book will cover much of the history of the oyster industry and oyster schooner but also demonstrate the present educational purpose of the *Meerwald* and the Bayshore Center. Another purpose is to stress the crucial importance of the waterways she calls home and the necessity of keeping healthy this lesser-known section of our otherwise heavily populated state.

Chapter 1

THE MEERWALD FAMILY
AND THE *A.J. MEERWALD*

Captain Ed Riggin returned home after World War I to find the town as prosperous and fancy as a gold rush town in the Old West. "Why them fellers looked like real dandies," he drawled, "with their white knickers and Cadillacs. One of them guys lit his 'ceegar' with hundred-dollar bills and traded in his Cadillac every time the ashtray got dirty....In them days we were doin' 6 and 7 million dollars' worth of business a year."[1]

It was a wild and raucous era—the Roaring Twenties. A few miles away, Nucky Johnson was running his Boardwalk Empire, the mob ran boats of illegal liquor in and out of the salt marsh and meadows and flappers and their escorts dined effusively on oysters. Oysters on the half shell, Oysters Rockefeller—oysters were in every recipe possible, and the industry made a boomtown of Port Norris and Bivalve, Cumberland County, New Jersey. The census for Port Norris shows over two hundred families, while a 1920 map of little Bivalve pictures fifty buildings, including a customs house, a pool room, a boardinghouse and two restaurants.

At the end of the decade, the Depression would hit southern New Jersey. The Delaware Bayshore would go from wealthy boomtowns to deserted wharfs, and the schooners that populated the Maurice River, filling the river with their graceful sails, would end as derelicts on its muddy banks.

THE MEERWALD FAMILY

Cumberland County, one of the southernmost counties in New Jersey, was blessed with two major rivers, the Maurice and the Cohansey, as well as a soil amenable to growing large crops of fruits and vegetables. While the inland portion of the county developed small cities profiting from poultry and egg production, as well as produce, in the coastal areas, many of the inhabitants along the Maurice River made their living on the water.

Port Norris was originally known as Dallas Ferry after Jonathan Dallas, who had established a ferry at that location. In 1810, Joseph Jones, known as "Coffee" Jones, inherited a great deal of money from his father, a coffee merchant, and began buying up tracts of land. He settled at Dallas Ferry and renamed it Port Norris after his son Norris.

Port Norris and Bivalve, on the west bank of the Maurice River adjacent to the bay, grew rapidly in size and importance because of the oyster trade. Writing in 1883, Cushing tells us that by the late 1800s, the area had become the chief oyster shipping market of the Delaware Bay with over 365 boats registered to oystering. Over 200 of these sailed from Bivalve, employing more than eight hundred men.

The heyday of the area's oyster harvesting began in earnest with the arrival of the Bridgeton and Port Norris Railroad in 1872, later to become the Cumberland and Maurice River Railroad after a bankruptcy problem. The road was completed in 1876 into Port Norris, with its main business being the transportation of oysters, from eight to fifteen carloads daily.[2]

When Augustus Meerwald came to settle in the area, it was to a very busy and profitable section of New Jersey. He was born in April 1833 in

The bugeye *Charles H. Gibson* was one of two boats owned by A.J. Meerwald Sr. The bugeye was a type of two-masted boat developed at the Chesapeake specifically for use in the oyster industry. *Bayshore Collection, gift of Sue Lane.*

Prussia, once a prominent state in Germany. He began work as a cabin boy on a ship sailing from Prussia to New York and, having arrived, jumped ship there.[3]

He eventually found his way down to Philadelphia, and in the 1860s, he traveled to Cape May County, buying "iron and bones" with the sloop *Pocahontas.* Later, he moved to South Dennis and built and commanded the sloop *Liffey* (built in 1871). The Meerwalds were devout Catholics, attending St. Elizabeth's of Hungary in Goshen. The senior Meerwald brought the church's building down to its site from Port Elizabeth in pieces on the *Liffey.* Meerwald planted oysters and made a good living of it. He and his son Augustus Jr. commanded two new boats, the sloop *Mary Meerwald* (built in Dennisville, 1891) and the bugeye *Charles H. Gibson* (built in Oxford, Maryland, 1876).[4]

A.J. Meerwald Sr.'s first wife, Margaret. All but one of her children had died by 1880, and Meerwald soon married his Irish maid. The couple had seven more children. *Bayshore Collection, gift of Sue Lane.*

Meerwald had two wives and numerous children. His first wife, Margaret, gave birth to Augustus Jr. and two other children, Mary and Joseph, who did not survive past their teens, dying of typhoid in 1877. She died in 1880 of typhoid. He remarried that year to his Irish maid, Mary A. Mulligan, who produced seven more children: Mary (Sister Mary Cornelius), Joseph A., Charles Joseph, (Father) John L., Willie, Margarite and Elizabeth.

But Meerwald Sr. himself was ill fated. News articles from June 1881 show he was injured while repairing his boat at Dennisville. He remained an invalid for the remainder of his life and died on June 30, 1903. His second wife, Mary Mulligan Meerwald Jeffers, was bequeathed all of his property and money. She remarried in 1905 and moved the family to Collingswood, but the family still spent the summer in South Dennis with their nieces and nephews from the first family.

Their son Augustus J. Meerwald Jr. was born in 1863 in Philadelphia and was married in 1895 in Goshen to Mary Agnes McCraven. The couple had eight children: Martha, Augustus Charles, William Augustus, Mary Agnes, Agnes C., Francis X., Edward John and Helen Margaret. All four girls were educated and became teachers, but it was expected that the four boys would follow their father into the oyster business. In the census records, Augustus

Left: Photograph of a painting of A.J. Meerwald and Mary Mulligan Meerwald (Jeffers). *Bayshore Collection, gift of Edward Tobin.*

Right: Captain A.J. Meerwald Jr. at the helm. The *Meerwald* was named after him by his sons Gus and Bill. *Bayshore Collection, gift of Sue Lane.*

Jr. is listed as a sea captain in the oyster industry, a successful oysterman and a well-known member of the Board of Shellfisheries. He also served on the Dennis Township Board of Education. Augustus Jr. and Mary raised their children in a home on County Road and Meerwald Road in South Dennis. An early boat owned by the Meerwalds was the *Martha Meerwald*, launched in 1909, also an oyster schooner, later owned and operated by Captain Fenton Anderson. The boat was named after their eldest daughter, a schoolteacher at the Eldora School in Dennis Township. Martha never married and lived across the street from her parents.[5]

THE SHIP THE *A.J. Meerwald*

It would be A.J.'s sons Augustus Charles "Gus" and William "Bill" who would eventually build today's schooner. Gus married Edna James, and they had one daughter, Gladys Meerwald Brewer, born in 1928. Bill married

Gus, Dick and Bill Meerwald are shown in 1920. Bill and Gus contracted with the Stowman yard to build the schooner they would name after their father, A.J. Meerwald. *Bayshore Collection, gift of Sue Lane.*

Florence Errickson, and they had two children, Florence Marie Meerwald Unkle Bright and William "Bink" Jr.

The boat would be built locally. Schooners built in the county were specifically tailored not only to oystering but to the particular needs of the local waters. The local shipyard in Dorchester, New Jersey, was established by Charles H. Stowman in 1890. Brothers Gus and Bill Meerwald contracted with the Stowman yard in 1928. The boat would be named after their father, Augustus Joseph. Gus and Edna mortgaged their home in Millville to raise money for the boat's construction. Bill Meerwald would operate the *A.J.* with his brother.[6]

According to Charlie Lofft in 1996, "She was built 57 Gross tons, 46 Net tons, 76.3 feet long with a beam of 22.1 feet and a hold depth of 6.3 feet." The *Meerwald* was rigged with a "Gloriana peaked" main sail, a foresail and a jib, otherwise known as a "bald-headed" schooner. Her equipment at the time included oyster dredging gear. "There is no evidence that there were any plans or specifications prepared and probably consisted of 'build one a little bigger than Joes' for $18,000." The *Meerwald* was one of the last sailing schooners to be built at Dorchester.

During the height of the industry, the cost of producing a schooner seems relatively inexpensive by our standards, but not in comparison to average annual salaries or by translating to today's dollars. In 1923, the schooner *Margaret Fowler* cost $25,000 to build, while a workingman earned $1,407 for an entire year. The *Ada Lore* cost $17,000 and the *Meerwald* $18,000. In 2020 dollars, these amounts would be $376,000, $258,000 and $274,000. In comparison, the *Meerwald*'s restoration in the 1990s cost $800,000.[7]

An article from the *Dollar Weekly News* featured the launching on Friday, August 21, 1928, at 11:00 a.m. at the Dorchester shipyard. She was christened by the youngest sister of Gus and Bill, Helen. The schooner is given as eighty-six feet long with a twenty-two-foot beam and equipped with a one-hundred-horsepower engine.

Gus and Bill operated the schooner *A.J. Meerwald* as an oyster boat for about five years. The boat was used for four and a half months per year during the spring planting season and operated out of Maurice River Village, New Jersey. According to the records of the Haskin Lab, in 1929, 2.2 million bushels of oysters were harvested in the area and as many as five hundred ships were registered oystering boats. In 1929, annual oyster sales amounted to $6 million and 4,500 people were employed for the bay season.[8]

LAUNCH OYSTER BOAT

There will be a boat launching Friday at 11 a. m., daylight saving time, at the shipyard of Charles H. Stowman & Son, at Dorchester, when the oyster schooner, A. J. Merwald, will take to her native element. This craft has been built for A. J. Merwald & Son, of South Dennis, and will be christened by the daughter of the former.

The schooner is 86 feet long and her beam is 22 feet. She is equipped with a 100 horse power standard engine, and will be used in the oyster business.

The schooner *Meerwald* was launched on August 31, 1928, as announced in this news clipping from the *Vineland Daily Times*. *Bayshore Collection.*

TROUBLED TIMES

Although the industry was booming, the *A.J. Meerwald* had a less than auspicious career. She had only been launched in 1928, yet one week after the start of the oyster season, an article in the May 7, 1929 *Vineland*

Oysterman Loses Life In High Gale

Report of Three Other Deaths gated by Officials by Officials

Reports that four men died at sea and three more were rescued after a three-day search, are being investigated by Federal officials at Bivalve today.

The crew of the oyster schooner A. J. Meerwald brought the story into port that one of their companions drowned at sea, and that three other sailors, who fell in at the same time were rescued.

Other oystermen related tales of a collision of two schooners in the Delaware Bay, off Port Norris, in which three men are reported to have died. Federal authorities are dubious of the report, but are investigating it.

The lost member of the Meerwald's crew was Calvin Spedden, Jr., 23, Cambridge, Md. His death was reported by the owner of the craft A. J. Meerwald, Millville.

The fatal accident occurred Friday during a high wind while Spedden and three other members of the crew were on the footchains reaching for the jib to set it into place. The four sailors fell into the bay and before a boat could be lowered Spedden had disappeared from the surface of the water. The other three men were rescued.

Instead of returning to port Captain Meerwald, together with other craft of the oyster fleet began a search of the bay for the body of Spedden.

The other accident is said to have occurred sometime Saturday.

All the oyster boats which returned to port over the week end report having "taken a bad beating" from the wind and high seas.

Daily Journal described the death of Calvin Spedden, age twenty-three, who was swept overboard during a gale. Other boats out on the bay at the time reported gale-force winds and heavy waves. Spedden and three other crew members were out on the chains (on the bowsprit) attempting to take in the jib when all went overboard. Three of the men were rescued by the others onboard, but although the *Meerwald* and other boats close by continued to search, Spedden was not to be found. His body was found a few days later across the bay at Lewes, Delaware, and claimed by his father, Calvin Spedden, a member of the Maryland State Tax Commission. Spedden Jr. left four sisters and one brother. Services were held at the home on Neck Road in Cambridge, Maryland, with burial at Greenlawn Cemetery. Spedden was one of more than one hundred men who would lose their lives working the water in the area over the years. A Watermen's Memorial Bell located at the Bayshore Center honors these men.[9]

The inquiry into the cause of death held on May 15 of that year found the captain to

Crew member Calvin Spedden was lost overboard and drowned during an intense gale. Spedden was only twenty-three years old. He had five siblings, of whom one sister may have been a twin. The Spedden family can trace their ancestry to the 1790s in Dorchester County, Maryland. *Bayshore Collection news article,* the Daily Journal *(Vineland), May 7, 1929.*

Captain Meerwald was found guilty of neglect in the accidental drowning of Spedden, having been warned that equipment was faulty and could cause a problem. *Bayshore Collection, Bureau of Statistics, State of Delaware, death certificate.*

be guilty of neglect and this to be a contributing factor in Spedden's death. "Cause of death as follows: accidental drowning by neglect of Capt. A.J. Meerwald, Jr. failing to provide proper equipment having been warned a weak hook holding foot rope would cause loss of life and failing to rescue or attempt rescue."

Not a good start for the *Meerwald* at all.

While the oyster industry was at its peak in the late 1920s, with plentiful spat indicating good harvests to come, the coming of the Great Depression in 1929 meant financial difficulties for some, and especially for Gus and Bill Meerwald. The industry was hit in the 1930s by the poor economy, overfishing, pollution and the growth of the population in the area creating runoff and muddying the waters to an extent that even the oysters could not cope. The entire oyster industry was seriously affected by the Depression, with the value of production dropping from over $3 million in 1929 to as little as $500,000 in 1939.[10]

The Meerwald family lost their boat to bankruptcy, as did others, and the impact of the financial crisis extended of course to the businesses dependent on the industry, such as shipbuilding, chandlers and the local stores and eateries. Additional damage occurred in 1938 when a notable hurricane struck the area of the oyster beds.

In the case of the *Meerwald*, the boat appears to have been used mainly through 1933 and spent a great deal of time simply moored at Dennis Creek. By 1935, her financial troubles were evident. The U.S. marshal sold the *A.J. Meerwald* at auction to repay creditors, including Gus and Bill's younger brothers, Francis and Edward, who had worked on the boat with them.

In the suit, Francis claimed an amount due of $7,220, while Edward asked for $3,935 on July 31, 1935. The amount actually awarded to the two came to only $1,343.86 in 1930s dollars. The schooner was purchased by the Texas-Pacific Realty Company, controlled by Benjamin Cohen, who put up $700 of purchase money, and a balance of $800 was paid to Cohen by Francis Meerwald.

The wives—Edna and Bill's wife, Florence—wound up purchasing the boat back at auction with financing from their parents. On October 4, 1935, Cohen sold the schooner to Florence and Edna for the sum of $1,700: $200 in cash, $800 by a note from Francis and Edward and the remaining $700 was mortgaged. At this point, Gus and Edna lost their home in Millville and moved to South Dennis, with her parents again throwing the lifeline by purchasing a home for them.[11]

The *Meerwald* sailing in 1929. The *Meerwald* was one of the "new style" boats developed expressly for use in the Delaware Bay area oyster grounds. *Bayshore Collection, gift of Francis and Edna Meerwald.*

In the meantime, the brothers gave up the seafaring life. Gus became an egg and poultry farmer, while Bill became a well-known justice of the peace and then magistrate for thirty-five years in Goshen. The boat itself lay inactive, tied up at Dennis Creek, having spent just a few short years oystering. Peculiarly, according to Gladys Meerwald Brewer, Gus's daughter, Gus was working on the boat at Dennis Creek at about this time. A man with a thick German accent came by and tried to convince him to sell the boat, but Gus demurred. Several days later, the FBI came by and told Gus that should he see the man again, he should sell it to him, as he was a German spy they were trying to catch![12]

In 1942, the boat was commandeered by the United States government. World War II made for a shortage of boats for the government, and it was a practice to offer reimbursement to owners for the use of a ship in the war effort under the Small Craft Requisition Authorization #115 of the War Shipping Administration. On June 1, 1942, an appraised value was set by the director of small vessel procurement of $12,498.

She was stripped of her masts and turned into a fireboat supporting ships loading munitions in the Philadelphia port. The ship was renamed by the U.S. Coast Guard as USCG-*86001-F* and used in the Philadelphia port until 1946. Two other local schooners were also requisitioned: the *Kathryn & Elma* and the *Emma & Ruth*. But even this "solution" would prove to have a downside.

According to Gladys Meerwald Brewer, Gus and Edna's daughter, the family had just begun to get back on its feet again and had put money into the boat's maintenance. But the government didn't necessarily see the boat as a prize. In November 1943, two representatives of the U.S. Maritime Commission, Loveland and Wood, reported, "The *A.J. Meerwald* has the reputation of being one of the poorer vessels requisitioned. It was learned after her requisitioning that the bow and part of the side planking of this vessel would need to be replaced." The commission maintained that she had been partially sunk and had been neglected by her owners. In May 1946, Flo and Edna were offered $10,700 for the boat, but they demurred.[13]

The Meerwalds were not happy with the compensation offered. Possibly due to the senior Meerwald's prominence, they did have friends. Senator William Barbour (Republican senator from New Jersey, 1931–37, 1938–43) wrote a letter on their behalf to Rear Admiral D.S. Land of the War Shipping Administration in Washington, D.C. "Statements made to me would seem to indicate that the offer made would work a very real hardship

Coast Guard fireboat *86001-F* in 1947, once known as the *A.J. Meerwald*, as she appeared during her days supporting munitions transfers on the river between Camden and Philadelphia. Her masts have been removed and a pilot house added, and pumps for water can be seen on the foredeck. This was only one of several major renovations the *Meerwald* would endure. *Bayshore Collection, gift of the photographer Robert Brewer.*

on the former owners of the vessel, I would appreciate your having a thorough investigation."

A series of correspondences occurred—to Flo Meerwald from the director of Small Boat Procurement, to one government office to another and, in July 1946, to the Meerwalds' lawyers, Stanger and Howell, from the Division of Small Boat Procurement.

It is not known what the admiral's reaction to the senator's plea may have been, but the boat was returned to the Meerwalds in 1947 with compensation of $13,200. Gus and a son-in-law, Robert Brewer, went to Riverbank, New Jersey, to accept the boat, having agreed to take her "as is, where is." "As is" must not have been a pretty sight, as Brewer said this was the only time he had ever seen Gus cry. Gus died in 1956. Bill, who had become a justice of the peace and municipal judge in Middle Township, died in 1963.[14]

Francis and Edward took up chicken farming successfully, earning a write-up in the local paper titled "The Meerwalds Find Success with Chickens." Edward died in 1988 and Francis in 1999. Francis served on the board of

W. WARREN BARBOUR
NEW JERSEY

General Files

COMMITTEES:
COMMERCE
MANUFACTURES
NAVAL AFFAIRS
PUBLIC BUILDINGS AND GROUNDS
RULES

United States Senate
WASHINGTON, D.C.

Answered 9/15/43
AEN

September 8, 1943 11340

My dear Admiral :

Several of my very close friends have
brought to my attention the apparent discrepancy in the
offer which has been made by the War Shipping Administration
and the computed value of the vessel "A. J. Meerwald" -
official number 227932, requisitioned June 1, 1942 - Req.
Aut. No. 115 which has been the subject of correspondence
between your Administration and representatives of the
owners of the vessel for some time.

I feel sure that a reasonable compromise
can be arrived at in this matter, but in view of the statements which have been made to me which would seem to indicate
that the offers made would work a very real hardship on the
former owners of the vessel, I would appreciate your having
a thorough investigation made to see if a fair and equitable
settlement might not be arrived at.

With appreciation for your cooperation, and
kindest regards

Most sincerely,

Warren Barbour

Rear Admiral Emory S. Land
War Shipping Administration
Washington, D. C.

Chairman's Office
Received: *9-10-43*
Sent Out

WWB
11

Above: A letter from Senator Barbour. The Meerwalds were unhappy with the
compensation offered them for the conscription of the ship and negotiated with the
Division of Small Boat Procurement. In September 1943, Senator Barbour (R-NJ) sent
a letter of support to Rear Admiral Land in Washington, D.C. *Bayshore Collection, U.S.
Department of Transportation, Maritime Administration Records (U.S. Maritime Commission and War
Shipping Administration, 1932–50).*

Opposite: On the dock in Bivalve are Jim Engle, Les Stauber, George Lemuth, Clyde Phillips
Sr. and Amos Pepper, 1939. *Bayshore Collection, gift of Clyde A. Phillips [Jr.].*

Jim Engle, Les Stauber, George Lemuth, Clyde Phillips Sr., Amos Pepper on dock at Bivalve 1939 ca.

the Vineland Egg Auction. Further generations of Meerwalds still reside in the area, and a road is named for the family. The schooner was kept in the family for two decades. In August 1947, the *Meerwald* was sold to Clyde A. Phillips for $30,000, along with two oyster grounds. Mrs. Phillips changed the name of the boat to the *Clyde A. Phillips.*

According to Clyde Phillips [Jr.], "Dad bought her after World War II after the [U.S. Coast Guard] sold her back to the Meerwald family. We got her about 1946 or '47. I was on her papers as captain right after high school and oystered with her. Best sea boat I've ever been on." Although the family sold the boat a decade later, ironically, Clyde A. Phillips [Jr.] would become one of those intent on the renovation of the *Meerwald* in the late twentieth century.[15]

For use as a fireboat, her masts had been removed and other mechanics had been installed. Phillips refitted her and put the ship back to oystering, but without her sails. During the war, the oystermen had lobbied the government to be allowed to oyster under power due to the dearth of crew members available. In 1949, a permanent pilothouse and larger engine were added to the *Meerwald.* The renamed oyster boat now went to work under motor and oystered for several years. At first, she was successful, selling sixty

The *Clyde A. Phillips*. After the war, the *Meerwald* was sold to Clyde A. Phillips and was used for oystering for several years. Though working under motor now, her masts remained in place. Piles of oyster shells are ready to be dumped back in the bay to encourage oyster growth. *Bayshore Collection, gift of Clyde A. Phillips*.

bushels of oysters on September 10, 1953, for $240. Pictures from those years show the *Clyde A.* loaded from gunnel to gunnel with oysters. Though working under motor, her masts remained, and the ship retained the look of the oyster schooner. Clyde Phillips Sr. died in 1957 and would never know what had ruined the oystering, but a year later, scientists would discover an oyster malady.[16]

Then the major blow hit. In 1957, the Delaware Bay oyster industry collapsed when a mysterious protozoan (single-cell organism) known as MSX (multinucleated sphere unknown) started killing oysters. Within two years, catches had dropped by 90 to 95 percent. The disease, now known as Delaware Bay disease, was introduced to the area by an unknown source, though scientists have speculated it was brought on the hulls of ships returning from the Pacific after World War II.

Imagine the oystermen pulling up their catch and finding nine in every ten oysters dead on arrival. The number of boat licenses for oystering went from 590 schooners and sloops in 1903 to fewer than 20 boats in 2020. Boats were changed over to clamming or "run up on the banks"—left as derelicts—as they and their owners ran out of steam and money.

The *Clyde A. Phillips* under motor. Mrs. Phillips changed the name of the boat from the *Meerwald* to the *Clyde A. Phillips* after her husband purchased the boat. *Bayshore Collection, gift of Clyde A. Phillips.*

At the death of Phillips Sr. in 1957, the boat was sold to first Harry Sharp, a Millville banker, and then the following year to Nicky Campbell and Albert Mollinkopf, who converted her to dredge clams. Clamming is a much different thing than oystering; oysters rest on the surface of the river or bay bed and can be raked aboard fairly easily. Clams, however, burrow into the mud, and a heavier dredge is needed to dig down and drag up the catch. Other changes included adding metal decking and sheathing the hull with metal. All of this would add ten tons of weight to the *Meerwald*. She served as a clammer for twenty years, at times operating on a twenty-four-hour basis. All of this would take a huge toll on the ship.

In 1965, the boat was sold to the East Coast Trawling and Dock Company. Then came a series of owners. An unrelated company called Clyde A. Phillips Incorporated purchased the *Meerwald* in 1977, but she remained idle. In 1983, the Phillips Inc. company merged with American Original Corporation of Maryland. The boat remained idle again until 1986 and was then sold to Donnie McDaniels of the New Sea Rover Company, who retired the vessel in March, and she languished at Eastern Marine in Salisbury, Maryland.

CORNELIUS CAMPBELL, 84

Oysterman

Cornelius S. "Nick" Campbell, 84, of Newport, died Thursday at home.

Before retirement in 1964, he was a self-employed oysterman in Port Norris. He owned and operated clamming boats in Atlantic City and Point Pleasant.

He was the former owner of the *Clyde A. Phillips*, which is being restored in Port Norris.

He was a member of the Newport Baptist Church.

Survivors include his wife, Bessie; a stepson, James Hollingshead of Millville; and two nephews.

Services will be held Sunday at 2 p.m. in the Hoffman Funeral Home, Port Norris.

Burial will be in Newport Baptist Cemetery. Friends will be received from 1 to 2 p.m. Sunday.

CORRECTION

Sears would like to clarify an ad running on the front cover of the December 18th Sears newspaper insert, as well as in the December Sears best customer bonus savings day direct-mail piece which you

Nicky Campbell purchased the *Clyde A. Phillips* and used her as a clammer, wearing her down physically. His obituary appeared in the *Daily Journal* (Vineland) on December 18, 1992. *Bayshore Collection.*

Donnie McDaniels started off oystering on his family boat the *C.M. Riggin*, which was owned by his grandfather Jacob Riggin. His grandfather and his brother Ed (*J&E Riggin*) also owned the *Charles Dolton*, *George Berry*, *Joan Jeffries* (*Nordic*) and *Helen Lois* (*J. Roberts Bateman*). Donnie was an oysterman for ten years, starting as a teenager. He would eventually buy out Ed's share of 1,500 acres of grounds at $1.50 per acre. When he had his first grounds, he planted three hundred bushels. In 1957, he planted five thousand bushels, and then MSX hit. In 1966, his grandfather died, so he got out of the oyster business.

"Five-dollar license and you were in [clamming] business," Donnie shared in a phone interview on September 18, 2020. Donnie was working for Clark Bean of American Clam Corporation at Maurice River. It was him who suggested to Donnie that he might buy the *Clyde A. Phillips*. He made the purchase in 1986 for $157,000 but never operated the boat. It remained in Salisbury, in McDaniels's eyes, obsolete. He made the purchase because the clamming license came with the boat. "I took the license to put on my metal clam boat, the *Yankee*." The *Yankee* is still clamming. In 1986, he sold the *Phillips* to John Gandy for $1.[17]

The ship Clyde Phillips names as "the best sea boat I've ever been on" was now a derelict. The once fabulously lucrative oyster industry on the Delaware Bay had been destroyed by not one but two marine diseases, as Dermo was still to come. During the Depression, several hundred boats were left to rot. The village of Maurice River has disappeared into the bank

Captain C.M. Riggin, owner of the *J&E Riggin* and *C.M. Riggin* and great-grandfather of Donnie McDaniels. *Bayshore Collection, gift of Harry Charles Gates.*

Prior to World War II, during the Depression years, the *Meerwald* was already in bad shape. *Bayshore Collection, gift of Olin McConnell.*

across from Bivalve, and Bivalve, Shellpile and Port Norris have become all but ghost towns, mere shadows of their former glory days.

Not all of the great oyster schooners met dire ends. Many oystered in the 1970s when oysters started to rebound. Some, like *A.J. Meerwald's* sister, the *Martha Meerwald*, continued to oyster until the early twenty-first century. The *Martha Meerwald* was built in 1909 and was a sixty-five-foot-long boat, nineteen feet wide. According to Fenton Anderson, she is built low to the water and carries a big load for her size. Anderson bought her in 1936 and converted her to power in 1945. When the change was made from sail, her bowsprit, booms and masts were all removed. Fenton says, "I didn't like it at the time, but it was necessary. Men went off to the war, and crews were hard to find. With sailboats, you put in terribly long days, up to sixteen hours a day. With a power boat, the longest day we have now is about eight hours."[18]

There are twelve schooners that survive, but nine are motor powered. These include the *Peter Paynter* (Essington, Pennsylvania, 1899), *Addie B. Robbins* (Greenwich, 1901), *C.J. Peterson* (Greenwich, 1908), *Howard W. Sockwell* (Leesburg, 1910), *A.B. Newcomb* (Greenwich, 1917), *John C. Peterson* (Greenwich,

On The "Martha Meerwald"

The *Martha Meerwald*, a sister ship, was also once owned by Augustus C. "Gus" Meerwald and named after the eldest daughter. *Bayshore Collection, gift of Sue Lane.*

The *C.M. Riggin* was one of the old oyster boats owned by the Riggins family. Her sister ship, the *J&E Riggin*, is now used as a Maine Windjammer taking tourists out for a sail. *Bayshore Collection.*

1927) and the *Dredge Monster* (1930). The *S.W. Sheppard* (Greenwich, 1922) now works the Long Island Sound and the *J. Roberts Bateman* (Greenwich, 1928) the Chesapeake Bay. The *J&E Riggin* and the *Isaac Evans* (*Boyd N. Sheppard*) continue to sail as part of the Maine Windjammer fleet.[19]

As Charlie Loft put it, "The *A.J. Meerwald* represents the peak of evolution of the design and construction of a vessel that has adapted, complemented, driven, and mirrored the gradual development, era of prosperity, and painful decline of New Jersey's Delaware Bay oyster industry."[20] Her eventual restoration and selection as the icon of the industry would give new energy to the bayshore.

Chapter 2

SCHOONERS AND SHIPYARDS

Today...the sound of the shipwright's cauling hammer is not heard very often. The rasping sounds of the adze and drawknife are stilled. There are no spars being soaked in water waiting to be stepped as new masts. Gone as well are the deadeyes, the lazyjacks, the throat halyards and marine hardware. Rarely is a sail ever seen along the marshy reaches of the Maurice River except in the memory of those "Old Gentlemen" who remember the forests of masts and the sight of countless dredgeboats tacking and beating to windward.
—*Donald H. Rolfs,* Under Sail: The Dredgeboats of the Delaware Bay: A Pictorial and Maritime History *(Millville, NJ: Wheaton Historical Association, 1971)*

*B*oats under sail were not only the mainstay of commerce on the Delaware but also gave heart to the towns of the lower bay and would become, in the end, the icon for the area. The schooner is a distinct style of ship, built differently here than elsewhere, and uniquely adapted to the shallow bays and coastal winds of southern New Jersey. The schooner was the backbone of the oyster industry in its heyday, and those who built her or sailed on her thought of her and spoke of her as family. Eventually though, ships under sail gave way to motors, wood to steel. As the industry began to fail in the 1950s, only a few of the wooden ships would survive.

The area around Port Norris was noted for the building of schooners as well as for the oyster trade itself. Shipyards and their shipbuilders were found up the rivers along the bay, and these local artisans created a unique schooner well adapted to the local industry.

BUILDING THE BOATS

While shipbuilding began in the colonial days on the Delaware Bay, sloops (single-masted sailboats) were the common style of ship used for the coastal waters at first and, in fact, were the boat used in the oyster business in the early 1800s.[21] Shipyards such as Mulford's and Myers' on the Maurice River produced sloops that ran the Delaware into the early 1900s. But our local shipwrights are said to have done their best work in the building of the schooner. These versatile and graceful ships were used not only in oystering but also in much of the local and international commerce. Coastal schooners traveled south to Cuba carrying local products and returned with exotic goods such as bananas and molasses. Inland, schooners traveled up local rivers bringing produce and lumber from southern New Jersey plantations into Philadelphia's port and served as couriers for personal and business mail. By the height of the oyster industry in Bivalve and Maurice River, the waterways were crowded with the schooner's distinctive rigging.

The author Joseph Conrad described the schooner poetically, capturing her innate grace: "They are birds of the sea whose swimming is like flying."[22] A schooner can be described as an open boat with at least two masts, with the foremast generally slightly shorter than the main, gaff-rigged (sails rigged from bow to aft) often with a jib sail. This type of rig was very usable for use along the coast due to the variable winds encountered near shore, and her shallow draft with centerboard up is ideal for the close-in travel, as well as for sailing into the nearby rivers such as the Cohansey and the Maurice. They are able to sail closer to the wind and are easier to maneuver in the narrow rivers and small ports of the area. The schooner became the go-to ship, not just in southern New Jersey, but all along the eastern and Gulf coasts. She was especially popular though with those areas supporting an oyster industry, such as Long Island, the Chesapeake Bay and, of course, the Delaware Bay.

The building of sailing ships was a continuing Cumberland County industry with several shipbuilding enterprises working in the nineteenth century and continuing well into the twentieth. A shipyard at Bridgeton, where two large schooners and sloops were under construction, is recorded

At first, the oyster trade relied on sloops for their business, but the schooner took over and became the go-to vessel in the industry. The sloop is smaller than the schooner and has only one mast. *Cumberland County Historical Society, photograph by Harvey Porch.*

in the 1838 census. Yards or companies for building schooners with three and four masts stood on the Maurice River at Leesburg, Mauricetown, Millville and Dorchester. Greenwich on the Cohansey was a site noted for the construction of oyster boats late in the nineteenth century.[23]

The first schooners favored for oystering had a clipper bow like those originating in New England and Maryland. These "old boats" were built until the beginning of the twentieth century. They were roughly fifty feet in length and noted by their high top mast and top sails. Built without engines, they were retrofitted later on. By the mid-1920s, local shipwrights had begun to build ships nearly twice the length of the old boats, favoring a spoon bow allowing for more deck space for their catch and adding a spike bowsprit. The "new boats" were adapted also to use a larger dredge for hauling up the catch and needed few men to handle the boat. A larger dredge equaled a larger boat overall. They were built with engines available to use during harvest season, though the law still allowed collecting seed oysters only while under sail. During the bay season, it was required to remove the propeller

The *J&E Riggin*, owned by Captain C. Riggin, Donnie McDaniels's grandfather, was a "new ship" similar to the *Meerwald. Photograph by R. Dolhanczyk of a painting in the Bayshore Collection by Charles "Chilli" McConnell (1897–1983).*

from the engine to avoid anyone cheating by using the motor. Each harvest season, the schooners would be refitted for power by removing the sails, gaffs and booms, installing a pilot house and reinstalling the propeller.[24]

The *A.J. Meerwald*, built in 1928, was one of these "new boats" built at Dorchester. "Diesel engines in the boats?—no not from the beginning. They were only sailing ships. Diesel engines were around from 1898. The *Meerwald* was built with power in the '20s—all of them did. First decade they could use power down the bay, but it was usually all sail. 1920 was when they started."[25]

Dorchester in the Maurice River Township is a small area on the Maurice River that has been a hub of shipbuilding since the land was purchased from the West Jersey Proprietors in 1799. The shipyard in Dorchester where the *A.J.* was built was established by Charles H. Stowman in 1890. Following his death, the yard was run by his sons, Charles A. and William B. Then in 1942, it was sold to the next generation, Walton G. Stowman, Frank Wheaton Jr. and Bennett Stowman. It survived the war by producing mine sweepers and in 1963 became Dorchester Shipbuilding, which is still in business. In the years from 1922 until 1931, the shipyard produced twenty-five oyster schooners for the industry.[26]

Stowman's shipyard in Dorchester, New Jersey, was once one of many in the county. It remains in business doing repair work on local ships. *Courtesy of Michael J. Chiarappa.*

At Dorchester, boats were built with double-sawed frames. According to Rolfs in *Under Sail*, local shipwrights believed that using steam to bend the frames damaged the wood, while the double-sawed technique extended the life of the boat. They were built of local white oak using a system called carvel planking, a method said to be more efficient than others. The planks are nailed or screwed to the frame of the boat, and then the seams are caulked. The planks do not overlap as they do in other styles of boat construction. Boats were built from a model distinct for each and then marked out on the floor at the shipyard. White oak and yellow pine were the woods of choice, and these were abundant around the Maurice River.[27]

Delaware Bay ships are designed first from half-hull models. Only two[28] were ever designed by naval architects. Half-hulls were carved from layers of wood, and the measurements for the ship were extrapolated to full size at the shipyard in a process known as lofting. This was the practice locally as late as 1983. "Master Shipwrights used imagination and design skill to carve a half-hull model from several layers of wood glued together into a block."[29]

The other industries came along—rigging, sail making, chandlery (supplier of equipment for boats) and so on—industries needed by the shipbuilding yards and the sailors. Along the shipping sheds in Bivalve,

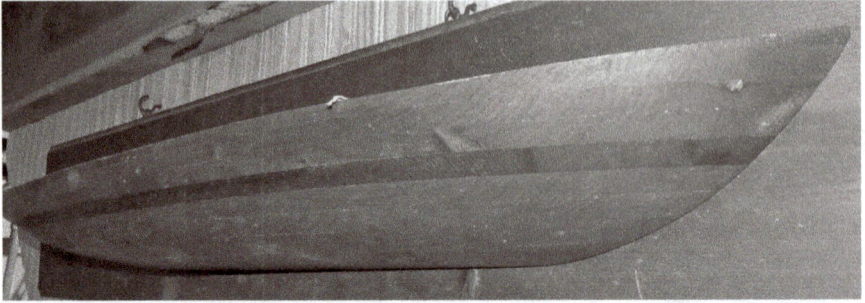

Half-hulls were carved from layers of wood and were used as the models to determine the specifics of the ship to be built. The half-hulls have become collectors' items now and can be found in museums as well. Hobbyists still create these to honor past ships. *Photo taken by R. Dolhanczyk of a half-hull, Bayshore Collection.*

compatible businesses lined the wharves—Hettinger Engine; Yates, Planter and Shipper; Berry's Meat Market; and Ed Cobb, Sailmaker.[30]

During the 1920s, distinctive stylistic developments took place in New Jersey to give the "new-style" schooners a definite Jersey look. According to Anne Witty, this was also when the builders lengthened the mast and increased the angle of the mainsail gaff. Newer boats were longer, averaging between seventy and one hundred feet in length rather than the roughly fifty feet of the old style, and were faster and more efficient than the old style. They were also easier for a crew to handle, so a boat could be run by two or three hands. Once the sails were hoisted, sailors could handle the dredge while the captain sailed the boat with some assistance for tacking. These boats also included a centerboard to replace a deep keel, again making the boat more suitable for shallow waters. The fact that they are wide and have a low gunnel makes it easy to hoist the oysters on board.[31]

In an oral history interview in 1983, local oysterman and clammer Harold Bickings said:

> *We feel they're probably the best thing around to catch oysters in Delaware Bay. The plank is two and a half inches thick—oak plank. I have a boat that was built back in 1914, and you can hardly pound a nail into her timbers, because they are that hard. It's easier to maintain them than to replace them, because what you would replace them with wouldn't withstand the vigors [sic] of dredging in the Delaware Bay. All these boats were built out of Jersey oak with Jersey cedar decking. And it's just the type of wood that lasts a long time. I think it's a testimonial to the workmanship of the people that originally built the vessels.[32]*

By 1904, businesses to complement the oyster industries lined the wharves along the shipping sheds. There were local businesses selling meat, making sails and repairing engines, as well as those that planted, harvested and shucked the oysters. This image depicts loading the train at the oyster shipping sheds. *Bayshore Collection, gift of Bill Biggs.*

Square timber blocks were used for the keel. These were set up at a slight downward slope, and the keel was laid on top of these blocks. A group of men worked to hew the curved timbers to set up the ribs of the schooner, while others worked on planking and another group installed decks and cabins and the like. Once the ship took shape, everyone chipped in to help with the caulking, which is pushing strands of oakum into the gaps between the ship's planks and sealing them to make the seams watertight.[33]

The masts were set into steps on the keel, with a coin placed underneath to make for fair winds and good fortune. Hulls were painted white to reflect the sun and because it held fewer maintenance problems than darker paints. The hulls were then striped with red, blue and yellow, though no one seems to know why this practice began.

Work in the yards didn't pay a great deal. The Dorchester yard paid $2.75 to $4.30 an hour, according to Clyde Phillips in an oral history interview,

The *Cashier* looking festive on the occasion of her 100th birthday. After World War II, oyster schooners were allowed to work under motor, and she is shown with a mast in place but also a pilot house, indicating she has been converted. *Bayshore Collection, gift of Robert Blackman.*

and the DelBay yard paid $4.00. More money could be had on board the ships oystering, but since this was seasonal, the yards sometimes provided off-season work for the men.

The ships of the oyster fleet worked through the first part of the twentieth century, oystering in both New Jersey and Delaware waters. The Delaware oystermen were known as "cornshuckers," as they generally were farmers as well, and the Delawarians denoted the New Jersey men as "sandsnipes" after the local shore bird.[34]

After the war, the ships were allowed to motorize for bay season. Once sails were removed from the oyster schooners, along with the masts, centerboards and bowsprit, a pilot house was added, which was for the captain's use. Switching from sail power was a welcome change, making it easier for the oystermen to maneuver the boat around the grounds. Some old-style schooners from the 1800s continued working, such as the *Cashier*, built in 1849 in Cedarville and owned in the end by the Bayshore Center. *Cashier* worked for 151 years of service and was one of the oldest working vessels in the country.

SCHOONER AS SOUL

Witty says the schooner has a life cycle from its building and launching through periodic renewals, to its eventually being "put in a coffin," which refers to sheathing the hull with metal to shore up the wood hull. After its use is over, it is simply run up on the bank to die, as is seen along the Maurice at Port Norris.[35]

The schooner's importance to its community is obvious in its use as a logo in the community of Port Norris and elsewhere in the Cumberland County area. The schooner is seen on the sign as you enter Port Norris, on the websites of its historic societies and municipalities and even on a fire truck.

The boats remain part of the family. Witty mentions a "curious aspect" of the Jersey schooner culture is an underlying belief by their sailors that the vessels are somehow animate, living creatures. This is fairly common in maritime communities and is explained by Fenton Anderson in an oral history interview in 1988: "Well, wooden boats they creak and they groan, do all the same kinds of things as humans do. That's one of the reasons they talk of the boat as being alive." In an interview in 1983, Fenton says, "A captain and a boat are probably one thing."[36]

In fact, most of the boats are named for either their captain or some family member, especially wives and daughters, as is the case with the *A.J. Meerwald*, the *Martha Meerwald* and the *Clyde A. Phillips*. Women also participated by christening the boats as they were launched.

Clyde A. Phillips of Mauricetown noted in an interview with the *Inquirer* when he was eighty-three, "It was an amazing thing to see. New Jersey boats had four corner sails, and they looked pretty under sail....I always say that around here, people were defined by their boats, and many boats were defined by their people."[37]

Being "put on the bank" was the last cycle of a schooner's life. She was repaired for years until such repairs became unfeasible, and then she was clad with steel to keep her going. When she finally could sail no longer, owners simply ran her up on the banks of the river and left her there to rot away. *Bayshore Collection.*

The *Cashier* was built in 1849 in Cedarville and worked as an oyster boat past her 100th year of service. Note the self-dumping dredge mounted on the side and automotive "finger-picking" culling machine on the deck. She was captained by George McConnell. She was docked at the Bayshore piers and for some years was pumped out on a regular basis. It was finally decided that neither the time nor the money was available to save her. *Bayshore Collection.*

One man known for local shipbuilding was John DuBois. He describes the process of building a boat: "You have filch lumber. You lay your vessel out from your model and then go to your filch pile [wood with bark on, just lap sawed]. You get your patterns, cut your frames, set your keel and build a boat. There's a satisfaction like an artist with a painting. You wind up with something finished, and you're proud."[38]

In an oral history interview, DuBois said, "They'd say, 'They hauled out Jim Cobb this mornin'.'" The ship and the person were almost considered as one, and a good boat was described as "smart."

In her dissertation, *"Smart Boats, Able Captains,"* M.R. Zorn Moonsammy finds that the boats in the Port Norris area were conceived as persons. She quotes John DuBois: "I first became acquainted with the *Isaac Evans* in 1932," and she mentions others gossiping about a boat as "dead down the Tuckahoe." Those involved in oystering ascribed human traits to boats and, at times, conversely "spoke of a man as a boat." To the folk of the area, the boats came to represent the local society, "representing its aspirations, its achievements, and its failures." The schooner became a metaphor for the specific and unique knowledge owned by those who worked the oyster industry. Moonsammy highlights those who speak of the "ribs" or "high

Main gaff

Main peak halyard

Main peak halyard

Mainmast

Spring stay

Fore peak halyard

Foremast

Delaware Bay Schooner
A. J. Meerwald
Detail of Rig and Sail Plan

Fore gaff

Fore throat halyard

Main throat halyard

Jib halyard

FORESAIL
(927 sq ft)

Jib lazyjacks

MAINSAIL
(1870 sq ft)

Main lazyjacks

Fore lazyjacks

Jibstay

Forestay

JIB
(765 sq ft)

Reef points

Jib downhaul

Main shrouds

Main backstay

Fore boom

Jibsheet

Jib club

Bowsprit

Main boom

Mainsheet

Foresheet

Fore shrouds

Fore backstay

Jibsheet

BOW

Bowsprit shrouds

STERN

Dredge rollers

Bobstays

Rudder

Centerboard

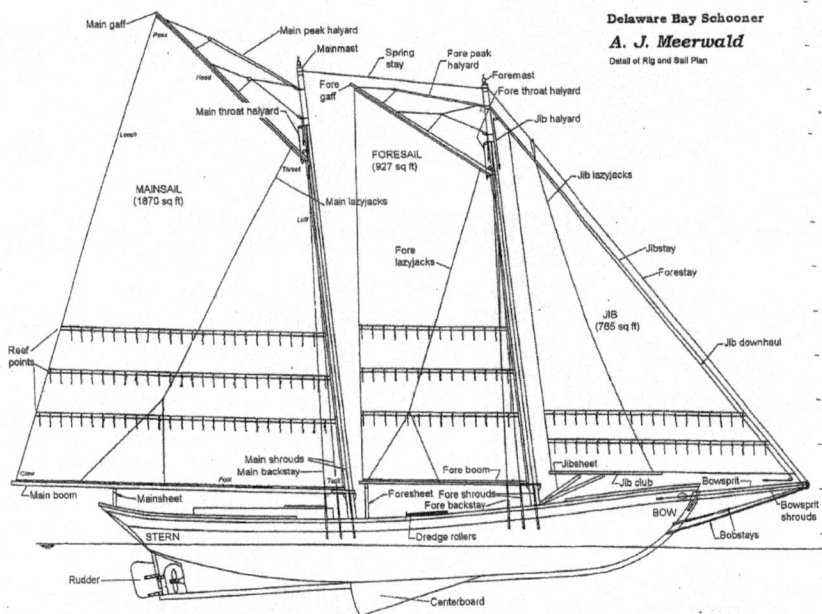

A drawing of the *A.J. Meerwald* showing details of her sails and construction. *Bayshore Collection.*

head" and personality of a boat. She quotes Captain Todd Reeves from an interview dated December 15, 1983: "If a boat don't do good, people think of you as you don't do good."[39]

THE CREW

The cook is often the crew member best remembered by the crew. It was he who prepared meals for them four times daily on a small stove in a very small space below decks. The work the men did out oystering was hard, and many calories would have been needed to keep up their energy. "We lived on the boat in the 1920 and '40s and we had a cook....We had a wood stove in the cabin. In order to have breakfast before sunrise, he had to have a hot stove. He'd start at 3:00 in the morning. We had ham and eggs and potatoes. We were well fed."[40]

Moonsammy says, "Local people often described the oyster crews as being hard drinking, storytelling, and raucous. In fact, 'boat stew,' the local

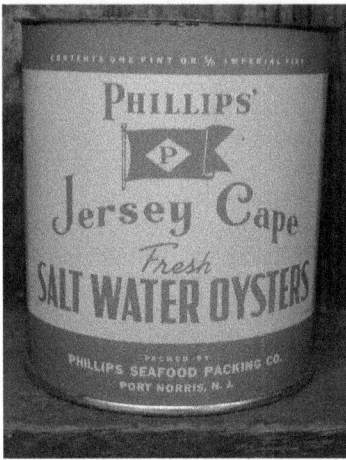

An oyster can from Phillips Seafood Packing Company. *Bayshore Collection, gift of Clyde A. Phillips.*

dish traditionally made on board for the crew on Mondays, was understood to be good to settle down a man's stomach after he had drunk a lot over the weekend."[41]

Most of those who worked on the boats began as migrant workers, as the shuckers did, but eventually stayed in the southern New Jersey area. On board the boat, the dredge was dragged along the reef and the oysters collected in the bag. The catch would be hauled in at first by a hand-winder and later by an engine. The dredge came up and over the roller and then dumped on the deck. Four men were assigned to cull or sort the oysters by size. "If you let it go too fast then the dredges will lift up off the bottom. If too slow, the dredge would dig in too far."[42]

Oystermen are farmers of the sea. The cultivation of oysters began in the nineteenth century. Seed oysters are transplanted to leased oyster beds and allowed to grow for three years before being harvested. So the oystermen plant, transplant and then harvest, just as with any crop. "You almost have to be born in the business to succeed in it because it's such a peculiar thing."[43]

Sometimes men worked independently on small boats. Lionel Hickman recounts, "It was hard work, very laborious work, sunup to sundown literally....I had a lot of family members who did tonging...and most of the time they got six to eight bushels....My father was a typical deckhand, which consisted of pulling the dredges in and culling the oysters while separating the oysters from their shells and stacking them."[44]

Boats under sail often worked the full week. Men were expected on board Sunday afternoon and returned on Friday. If you had no wind, you had no work. Once the boats worked under power, they would come back to port every night. John DuBois says, "I think wages was eighty dollars a month for these people."[45]

One of the main changes, though, was the installation of the pilot house, changing the graceful lines of the open oyster boat under sail. Bowsprits left, masthead figures disappeared and the boats were handled by fewer men, allowing for fewer hands available for maintenance. The traditional white hull with striping gave way to dark colors, and most local boats became dark green with occasional trim, giving rise to the nickname the "Green Fleet" for the Dorchester yard boats.[46]

Anderson bought the *Martha Meerwald* from Augustus J. Meerwald Jr.; it was built in 1909 and named after Meerwald's daughter. "I bought her in 1936 and converted to power in 1945. When we changed her from sail, we removed the bowsprit, booms, masts."[47]

According to Donald Rolfs (narrating the documentary *Schooners*), "New Jersey built the most beautiful ships ever seen." Fenton Anderson adds, "It's the fact you created this thing. There's other compensations besides the money."[48]

Not all of the boats are gone, though many are lying derelict along the banks of the Maurice. Some eight of the original schooners are still in use oystering, minus their sails, mechanized and modernized, but the best known of Jersey schooners, the *A.J. Meerwald*, is a stirring sight as she plies her trade as the icon of a bygone era. While many were sunk and discarded during the Depression or as disease struck the industry, some were resurrected. According to Anderson, the *Mattie Flavell* was abandoned in 1933, but "she's still living." The *Flavell* was purchased, refitted and, as of the 1980s, was oystering in Delaware.[49]

Two still in existence today were saved by Mainers looking for windjammers to sail in their tourist areas. The *Isaac H. Evans* was abandoned in Mauricetown and subsequently purchased for the Maine tourist trade. Originally built in 1883 as an old-style schooner, she is 58.8 feet in length on deck with a 19.5-foot beam (width). The *Evans* is still sailing from Rockland, Maine. Linda and Douglas Lee remembered, "We came down looking for a boat for charter." They bought the *Evans*, raised the deck 3.0 feet, rebuilt the stern and topsides and had her sailing within a year. "Only economic way to do it was to rebuild an old boat."[50]

The *J&E Riggin*, built in 1927 as a new-style schooner, is eighty-nine feet long with a twenty-two-foot beam. According to Rolfs in *Under Sail*, the boat was never beaten in a race. She won the first and only Great Delaware Bay Schooner Race in 1929. "My gosh," said Captain Riggin, "it was almost as if she was a live creature a-rising up out o' the sea, runnin' before the wind, a-goin' wing on wing." Frank Hinson adds, "Take a little breeze of wind and you would just have to reef her down to nothing to hold her dredges on the bottom."[51]

The *J&E Riggin* no longer oysters but was taken to Maine, where she carries passengers as part of the Maine Windjammer fleet. Both the *J&E Riggin* and the *Isaac H. Evans* were designated National Historic Landmarks in 1991.

All of this made it even more important to undertake restoration of the *Meerwald*. If the Jersey schooners would change with the times, it became crucial to save at least one boat to operate under sail, holding as true to her original lines and tradition as possible—something to show the past glory of the fleet. That ship would be the *A.J. Meerwald*.

Chapter 3

RESTORING THE *MEERWALD*

I told her at the first public meeting that she should change the boat's name back to the A.J. Meerwald *because the boat* Clyde A. Phillips *was never a schooner.*
—*Clyde Phillips, 2008*

I want to restore her as authentically as possible to help preserve the maritime heritage here, a lot of which is being lost. Most people don't realize there is a heritage on the South Jersey shore.
—*John Gandy, quoted by Joe Daly in the* Philadelphia Inquirer, *August 11, 1989*

Gandy's wish became a reality some years later. Many volunteers would work both on the ship and in the background to make it become a reality. The *Meerwald* would come off that muddy bank and become the symbol of the oyster industry.

In 1986, the *Meerwald*, known at the time as the *Clyde A. Phillips* and geared for clamming, lay on that mudbank near Salisbury, Maryland. John Gandy, Merchant Marine ship's captain and Mauricetown resident, purchased the boat and brought it back to New Jersey. He and a partner came across a barmaid with a passion for tall ship sailing who also had experience working in a shipyard, and they created the Delaware Bay Schooner Project, headed by Meghan Wren. Soon there would be a hodgepodge of workers—skilled shipwrights, retired mariners, volunteers who had no experience with ships and those who did, some local and some a few hours' drive away. Weekend work parties would bring all kinds of people together with one mission: to restore one of the oldest original oyster schooners in the bay area. Armed with 501(c)(3) designation and a submission to the State and National Register of Historic Places, and with a series of fundraisers and grant applications, the money was raised. Beyond any reasonable expectations, within eight years, the rechristened *A.J. Meerwald* was launched.

The Early Days

The spur for the restoration came about slowly. Donnie McDaniels began oystering on his family boat, the *C.M. Riggin*, as a teenager and continued for ten years. He said in a 2006 interview for the Delaware Bay Museum, "The history goes back to my great-grandfather Charles Riggin. He had the *Amelia Riggin*, the *J&E Riggin* and the *C.M. Riggin*." Eventually, McDaniels would buy his uncle Ed's share of 1,500 acres of oyster grounds.[52]

In 1957, he planted five thousand bushels of oysters, and then MSX hit. A disaster for the entire industry, the virus wiped out 90 percent of the oyster crop that year, and McDaniels got out of the oyster business and into the clamming business. Over the years, McDaniels worked for the Robbins Brothers, Gorton's of Gloucester and Campbell's Soup.

In early 1986, McDaniels bought the *Clyde A. Phillips* from the American Clam Corporation for $157,000. However, he never operated the boat at all. "The boat stayed in Salisbury, Maryland, obsolete." Donnie bought the boat for the clamming license in order to upgrade to a larger boat, the *Yankee*.

John Gandy studied nautical science with a minor in international studies at the University of South Carolina but then joined the navy and afterward the coast guard. After getting his second mate's license in 1980, he went to work sailing for Mobil Oil but always had a fondness for the oyster business in spite of seeing his grandfather working too hard and still not making enough money in the industry. Gandy bought a work boat called the *Flora Bell* from George Gaskell and took over Gaskell's oyster grounds. As merchant sailing is a three-months-on and three-months-off job, he would run oysters whenever he wasn't at sea. His wife, Rona, went along and culled the oysters.

In a 2019 interview with Rachel Dohanczyk of the Bayshore Center, Gandy describes discussions with Donnie McDaniels around 1986. "Whenever I'd see him…I'd say, 'Donnie, what are you going to do with that old oyster boat?' I always had the idea how great it would be under sail." The local Dorchester shipyard had hauled out a one-hundred-foot schooner recently,

Arnie Robinson, Meghan Wren, Charles Lofft, Bob Dunlap and Rona Gandy. The occasion is the purchase of an office building and the first of the shipping sheds in 1995. *Bayshore Collection.*

and the schooner's launch had impressed him. Gandy said, "She went down the river under full sail, and she was hardly making a ripple the hull was so well designed."

"I was just kinda joking with Donnie. Finally, we were walking along and I brought it up again. He said, 'John, you want it bad enough.' He made me an offer I couldn't refuse. One dollar. Sight unseen. Then I thought, holy cow, what am I going to do? This was the *Clyde A. Phillips*. I didn't know Clyde at the time. I knew she'd been built in Dorchester, so I knew what kind of boat she'd be."

His wife, Rona, added, "From the time we were in college, I heard him talking about the old oyster boats under sail, so I wasn't at all surprised."

Now that he owned the oyster boat, he and his fifteen-year-old son, Nathan, drove three hours on weekends to a small creek west of Salisbury to work on her. She was floating, but only with three pumps going. The two would go aboard to hear where the loudest sound of the water was and then get down into the water to caulk the seams. But Gandy said, "I don't think we accomplished a thing. You know how it is walking in mud. Imagine an eighty-five-foot boat sitting down in the mud, and as the tide rises, she comes back up; you can imagine the suction. So she probably didn't have much caulking left."

The Gandys continued their caulking efforts for about a year and then met Steve Carnahan from the schooner *Pioneer* when it came down to Bivalve. The *Pioneer* was an educational boat operating out of New York Harbor. Gandy considered himself fortunate when the captain, Dianne Glennon, mentioned they were shorthanded for a week-long cruise to the Chesapeake. He ran home and got his things. That cruise focused his thinking, and he was now torn between doing a nonprofit similar to theirs or possibly a business.

As John Gandy and Steve Carnahan discussed the boat project at Greenwich Boat Works, an apprentice, Meghan Wren, came over to ask about the project. Later that evening, Gandy and Carnahan would run into Meghan at the Ship John Inn, where she bartended. Gandy would meet with her again, and she would work for him on the haul-out of his own boat, the *Flora Ball*.

Meghan Wren was a Millville girl who, having spent her summers at the Jersey shore learning to sail and exploring mud flats, was equipped with a

Meghan Wren found her experiences sailing on tall ships fulfilling, and when she realized that there was a historic sailing ship in need of restoration, she jumped on the chance to participate. She would become the executive director of the Bayshore Discovery Project for thirty years and lead what was once the Schooner Project to restore not only the *Meerwald* but the shipping sheds and the local culture as well. *Bayshore Collection.*

variety of skills not common to many young women. These included some unique skills needed for the restoration of a schooner.

After a post-grad year at the Peddie School and one year at the University of Pennsylvania, Wren had packed a tent and her dog and set out to see the world, or at least the United States. Eventually, she landed on the "Tall Ship for Texas," sailing to the 1986 tall ship celebration for the Statue of Liberty. The "authenticity" of the ship, the *Elissa*, lay in her basic construction— wood, canvas sails, hemp lines—and Meghan felt that "her aura of quiet power seduced me." She found the experience of sailing a tall ship mesmerizing and fulfilling. Back home in Cumberland County, she would find work shipbuilding as well as bartending.[53]

As she listened in on the conversation between Gandy and Carnahan, she sensed an opportunity. Here was a historic sailing ship in need of TLC, a ship that was part of the Delaware Bayshore region and one she felt could be restored and would celebrate the cultural heritage of the community—at the time, a heritage largely ignored. "She wasn't one of the more talked-about ships as she'd been laid up too long, but she was representative of the Dorchester type of schooner."[54]

While Gandy was still debating between developing a nonprofit or a for-profit organization, Wren would push for the former. "I had wanted to do something in the way of an educational boat, and here they were talking about the same thing, so I kind of asked if I could help."

First in importance was to bring the boat back to Bivalve from the Chesapeake. Carnahan knew someone with a tugboat who could bring the *Phillips* up to the Delaware. Gandy couldn't go along, as he was working at the shipyard at the time, so Steve and Bob Jackson went. Gandy took off and came to Bivalve to watch her come in. "It looked like a fire boat—jets of water with pumps running continuously. The tug was pushing a barge and had the *Phillips* tied to the barge, and he was going full throttle."

Rona Gandy recalled meeting Meghan Wren: "The first time I met Meghan was when they towed the boat into Port Norris. I didn't know she was a champion swimmer when she jumped off with the line and swam to shore to secure it to a tree."[55]

At the time, Wren signed on as a shipwright's apprentice to Clem Sutton of Greenwich Boat Works for a couple of years. Sutton also had properties in Millville, and Wren worked as a handyman for him as well. It was, according to Wren, an incredible learning experience. Gandy, in the meantime, had

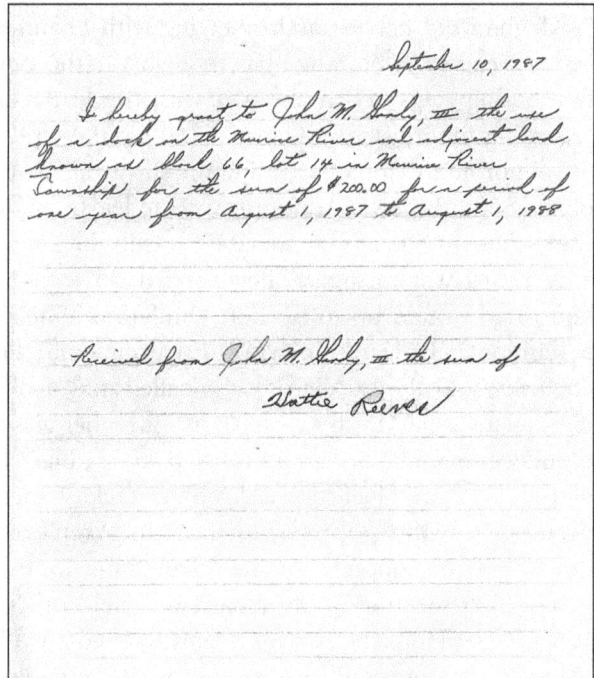

The agreement with Hattie Reeves. The Schooner Project rented a dock at Penny Hill from Reeves for $200. It gave the early project a place to work but proved to have some problems, and the ship sank three times before they were able to haul her out. *Courtesy of John Gandy.*

gone back to work at sea, and Carnahan and Bob Jackson brought the *Phillips* up to Port Norris. It was part of Meghan's job to check on the boat daily.

Gandy had arranged with Hattie Reeves, who had a dock at Penny Hill in Maurice River Township, to rent it for $200 a year. There was no electricity; the nearest was at a dock near the Mauricetown bridge. Gandy asked if he could run electric cable even though it was quite a distance away—Gandy estimates maybe three hundred feet. "I bought electrical cable like you would wire a house and put a heavy-duty grounded plug on one end and a receptacle on the other. There were a couple of boats tied up where the old bridge used to be, and I got permission to plug into their power."

THE SCHOONER PROJECT

"We had started talking to people. People thought it was a great idea, kind of foolish, and pitied us. As bad as the industry, the economy was so poor, but then we started to have fundraisers and get the word out….A lawyer, Bob Dunlap, agreed to do the work on the 501(c)(3) pro bono, and the *Phillips* nonprofit corporation was formed, transferring the ownership of the boat to the entity."[56]

Meghan did her research, meeting with Dianne Glennon of the South Street Seaport, who was able to help on the development process and fundraising steps. Then she met with the leadership at Wheaton Village regarding fundraising in Cumberland County and took the paperwork for the nonprofit to Trenton. In addition, she would meet with Steve Applebaum of the Small Business Administration to learn about keeping the books and start school at Stockton State College with the idea of getting a degree.

A board was formed. They needed three people to be incorporated, and these wound up to be Bob Dunlap, a Vineland attorney; Al Huber, a retired DEP (Department of Environmental Protection) hydrographic engineer; and Roger Allen, the so-called mayor of Bivalve and curator of the Philadelphia Maritime Museum. Al Huber was a major force, especially in fundraising. Huber had a license plate reading "Oyster" that is now part of the Bayshore Collection. Al took a stack of forms and came back with twenty-five members for the organization. Wren would become the executive director of the nonprofit and its driving force for thirty years.

The first meeting of the board was held on November 2, 1988, with Wren, Greg Honachefsky, John Gandy, Clyde A. Phillips [Jr.], Joe Walton, Dave Rutherford and Rona Gandy in attendance. According to the

The *Meerwald* in need of restoration. Actually, at this point, she was the *C.A. Phillips,* just moved up from Salisbury in hopes of restoration. *Bayshore Collection.*

minutes, bylaws were completed and attorney Dunlap agreed to establish the 501(c)(3). They would meet the first Wednesday of each month. The first member to sign up would turn out to be none other than Clyde A. Phillips [Jr.]. On December 7, they acquired the first fifty dollars in the treasury and determined they would issue a quarterly publication. Dues for membership would be twenty-five dollars. Each member would be obligated to sell twenty tickets by March 1989 for their first fundraiser, a banquet. Within one year, they would have over 90 members of the Schooner Project. By 1993, that number would have risen to 450, not all active to be sure, but dues-paying nonetheless.[57]

Not all went smoothly. The boat would first sink a month later when power was lost to the pumps. Gandy says, "She sank and the fire company came—they were wonderful."

Above: Rick Waters and Milt Edelman, shipwrights, working on the restoration. *Bayshore Collection.*

Left: The shipyard at Dorchester did a haul-out in 1988 to no avail, caulking the ship up to the waterline for $6,393—a good price, probably since Gandy had a working relationship with them. However, the Schooner Project did not have the money at the time and hustled to put together their first fundraiser. *Courtesy of John Gandy.*

The first business of restoration was to stabilize the boat and keep her from sinking. This was accomplished by using bilge pumps to keep the ship afloat. Gandy convinced the Dorchester shipyard to haul her out even though there was no money to pay for the $6,393.34 bill. The haul-out at Dorchester caulked the ship just to the waterline, so it was up to the volunteer crew to try to lighten up the ship and get her caulked above the waterline.

A news article by Joe Daly in the August 1989 *Inquirer* says, "John Gandy is at work on a restoration near Mauricetown. His focus is the *Clyde A. Phillips*, one of the last of the original wooden twin-masted oyster schooners. While it was not much to look at in 1989, Gandy could see the lines of the schooner and brought it home from Maryland where it lay in the mud a derelict. Gandy established a nonprofit organization, the Clyde A. Phillips, Inc. to help fund its rebirth."[58]

> *Early December* [1989], *right about Deer Week…we had a blow-out tide, two blow-out tides in a row, and she was sitting in the mud at her mooring and had kind of a little hole where the bow sat at low tide, and when she got a real low tide, you know, it went further down.*
>
> *I got a telephone call from a reporter, saying, "So what do you have to say about the boat being sunk?" And I said, "Well, that was in '88 and… you know, everything's fine." And he said, "Well, I'm talking about today." I hung up pretty quickly and dashed down.*[59]

When the ship had sunk before, the fire company had come out and helped raise her by pumping the water, but Wren knew there was little hope they would come out that week, as the local fire companies were out in the woods for Deer Week (a local deer hunting tradition). Pumps were gathered from various sources, and she was brought up again. Wren mentions a number of people who worked to bring her up. Greg Honachefsky; Ezra Cox, owner of Penny Hill Marina; Al Huber; and others worked to borrow pumps up and down the waterfront. "We kept adding pumps until we got her up."

Now it was clear they needed to haul her out again in January 1990. This time, the bill would be $11,000 for removing the pilot house, plank replacement, caulking and bottom painting. But even this was only partial work, and much more would need to be caulked before the *Phillips* would be able to float.

Four months later, she was moved to Leesburg, towed by the *Howard W. Sockwell*. The third attempt brought into focus the problem. The idea of the restoration needed to become a reality, as the *Phillips* was in worse shape

The *Meerwald* on the work site. Using a 275-ton crane, the ship was set on the bank at Penny Hill in February 1992. Restoration would continue at this site without further fear of the ship sinking, as she had three times already. This is one of the first haul-outs intended to stabilize the ship by removing the excess weight of the steel reinforcements from her clamming days. *Bayshore Collection.*

than before she sank and was in jeopardy of sinking again. But Gandy had gone back to sea and wouldn't be able to operate the restoration process. "I was hooked at this point," says Wren, "so why not let me do the nonprofit education concept, having it be a cause instead of a business—and he agreed."[60]

A volunteer membership began to form, and work parties were scheduled. Eventually, there would be paid shipwrights on the job who would supervise the volunteers who would remove planks and do the heavy work. The work parties continued, and one volunteer would recruit another.

David Rutherford, a retired city planner and dairy farmer from Cape May Point, was one of the first to join in. He would prove invaluable as they fought to keep water out and make the ship tight again. Rutherford attended the first meeting and then joined the next work party and kept coming every weekend for the next three years as the ship was prepared for

John DuBois, Meghan Wren and John Gandy in front of the ship under restoration, October 8, 1988. *Bayshore Collection.*

haul-out. "We had the dilemma of letting daylight into the hold without the accompanying rain and weather coming too. Dave said, 'I got this,' and designed and built a greenhouse structure to be a 'lid' for the main hold hatch."[61] While Rutherford left the project once the boat was hauled out and on its way, many years later, he would bequeath $250,000 to Bayshore Center.

Chuck Pritchard of Cape May was introduced to the project by David Rutherford. Chuck was into "boats, wooden boats, just the whole thing."[62] He had previously built a Delaware Ducker and a Melon Seed, two types of traditional small craft native to the area—light enough to work in the marshes but seaworthy in the rougher bay as well. Chuck and his wife, Hilary, had moved to Cape May in the mid-1970s to open the popular gift shop the Whale's Tale and were part of the revitalization of that shore town. Rutherford said, "There's this young woman....I know you love wooden boats, and this will be of interest to you." They went to a project meeting at the Union Hall and began to volunteer regularly. Pritchard would also bring in Jim Albertson, a local folk singer.

Merv Willis, a retired naval architect, would bring in his friend and colleague Charlie Lofft, a retired marine engineer, and the two would work

David Rutherford, from Cape May Point, was one of the first to join the project and then joined the work party, proving invaluable for more than three years. He would later remember the *Meerwald* in his will. *Bayshore Collection, 1990.*

to meet the U.S. Coast Guard regulations. Merv did the line drawings and stability calculations by hand. The paperwork that needed to be submitted to the coast guard was a lot, so he brought in Charlie to help. Charlie's navy background included shipbuilding. According to Wren, "He quickly grew from BDP's [Bayshore Discovery Project] marine engineer to our chief procurement officer, operations committee chair, trustee and then chair of the board."[63] Lofft would search for needed gear for the boat and also be responsible for the federal documents needed. Besides the normal requirements of getting a boat in the water, they would also need to meet USCG standards, the secretary of the interior's Standards for Historic Preservation and eventually the state and federal grant guidelines. "She's beautiful," he said. "She has a pretty line to her. There's just something about her," Lofft told Joe Daly in an interview for the *Inquirer* in 1989.

Chuck Pritchard then introduced his friend Milt Edelman to the project. Milt would become the head shipwright, providing expertise to the work. Edelman, a shipwright by profession, was another Cape May resident who would be integral to the restoration of the ship. Friends with the Pritchards, he attended the first fundraiser with them. During the early years of the project, the volunteers "built comradery and support, but not much work was done."[64] They removed the clam gear and enjoyed being together. Then

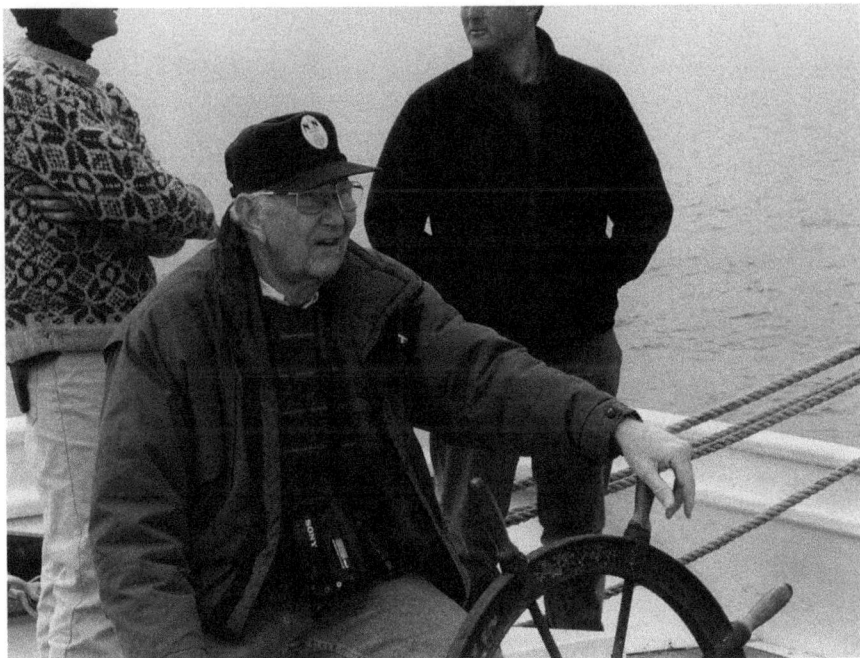

Charlie Lofft, project director and board president, became somewhat of a jack-of-all-trades, bringing his navy background in to help with coast guard paperwork, among other chores. *Bayshore Collection.*

the boat sank, and the Roseman Boatyard got the *A.J.* floating again. There were many who thought that would be the end of her. The focus had to be, according to Edelman, "not to build a better boat, but the same boat," or in other words, to ensure she was authentically restored. Milt would bring his mentor, Mort Hughes, to the project.

Key volunteers included Knute Asenberg, David Rutherford, Mort and Millie Hughes, John Parlapiano, Dee Curriden, Mike Chiarappa, Greg DeCowsky, Bob Gallant, George Wille, Charlie Elmer and Greg Honachefsky. The Hugheses would spend their weekends in Bivalve in their RV while Millie cooked for everyone. It was up to Mort and Milt to manage the volunteers. Asked how many, Edelman says, "God, it was a gang of people."[65] Mike Chiarappa, a PhD and professor of history whose work focuses on environmental and cultural history, would be responsible for measuring all of the planks on the bottom of the boat and keeping good documentation. Milt himself kept daily work logs, which are kept in the Bayshore Center's archives. According to Milt, "The best part of the organization was the volunteers." These were not local people for the most

Many volunteers worked on the ship. Here, the 1992 haul-out crew is lined up on a cold winter's day. *Bayshore Collection*.

part; they were from other parts of New Jersey and Delaware. They would come down and stay in hotels just to work on the ship.

Mort Hughes showed up and contributed his knowledge of shipbuilding. Meghan remembers one Saturday when a Winnebago pulled up and an older man got out and came aboard. At the time, they were desperate to remove some of the weight from the ship. The steel masts and the surf-clamming rig had been added, and these were keeping the boat lower in water, exposing some of her worst seams. Mort, the owner of the Winnebago, finally spoke up: "You don't need money. Just get a ladder, a cutting torch, some chain, a shackle and a few strong backs."[66]

According to Mort's daughter, Suzanne Benoit, "My dad remembered the *Meerwald* when it was first built in 1928 when he was a small boy, and that's one reason he was so involved. He was a shipwright and welder and did some blacksmithing to make some of the metal rigging on the *Meerwald*. He used his dad's portable forge."[67]

The following weekend, Meghan recalls the group watching and doing the grunt work as he cut the mast down, bit by bit. Over fifteen tons of steel were removed from the hull, as well as numerous other extraneous items, which improved her watertight integrity and prepared them for the

Mort Hughes removing the clamming rig. Hughes directed the removal of the metal clamming gear, over fifteen tons of steel, including the steel mast. He confessed that he had fabricated and installed it years earlier. *Bayshore Collection.*

rebuilding phase. "Mort let us in on the fact that thirty years earlier, as a welder in Cape May, he personally had fabricated and installed that steel clam mast on the *A.J.*!"

Still, the organization was in debt before it even began. At one point, Wren and Honachefsky slept on the boat, setting an alarm every hour to make sure the pumps kept working. Afterward, they moved, and she continued to tend bar while he worked as a game warden, and between them, they paid for the electric at the dock and filing fees. Fundraising would be crucial.

Rona Gandy was asked to be the volunteer coordinator. "It was a lot of people like me who didn't know which end of the boat was which, and there was no money and everything had to be done. We took old planks from the ship so people could buy them as souvenirs and collected spikes to sell."[68]

Others volunteered, such as Mark Stellinberger, a local game warden, and Joe Butler, owner of a bed-and-breakfast in Cape May. An important factor was the inclusion of the press. Joyce Vanamen of the *Atlantic City Press* and Jean Jones of the *Bridgeton Evening News* got out the news for them. Larry Sarner, chief educator for the New Jersey Fish and Game, developed the Project Aquatic Wild Curriculum for the Bayshore Center and helped the center receive a DEP award, giving the project credibility in the education field.

Mort Hughes working underneath the reframed *Meerwald* during the restoration. *Bayshore Collection.*

For their first major fundraiser in April 1989, they worked with local artists. Al Huber had meetings with people on the boards of local hospitals and the bank. Wren recalls, "He knew people and called in a lot of favors." They would auction art and art lessons and donations of all sorts at a dinner at the country club. Pat Witt of the Barn Studio was instrumental in gathering over two hundred pieces of art to be auctioned, a testament to the amount of interest the restoration was incurring in the area.

"The night before the event, we had nothing written, no program," Rona Gandy remembers. "I had never run a computer but could type, and here we are with this little office computer on Main Street. Meghan handed me all this stuff and said put the program together. We did what it took—if it took until two in the morning, that's what we did."[69] That first fundraiser, the Oyster Dinner and Art Auction at the Cohansick Country Club, would net $9,000, a good start toward erasing the debt but nowhere near what was needed. Later fundraisers would include a benefit cruise on the Cape May Ferry with dinner in September 1989, the annual Bay Days event in June and a spring walking/running race through Bivalve and

Port Norris. Artists Connie Jost and Glenn Rudderow painted murals for the Delaware Bay Museum, and artist Ray Thorley painted the *Meerwald* under sail. Prints of the painting were sold to raise funds. Knute Aspenberg crafted a detailed model of the schooner and donated it to the cause. Internationally renowned glass artist Paul Stankard donated a piece for the art auction.

Rona Gandy would continue to volunteer and, in fact, took her husband's seat on the board while he was at sea. At that time, everything was about getting the boat rebuilt; the stage of planning how the ship would become an educational force was yet to come.

Progress on the restoration was painfully slow, and the many fundraisers only provided a fraction of what was needed to complete the work. But Wren felt their credibility was established simply by the fact that they didn't

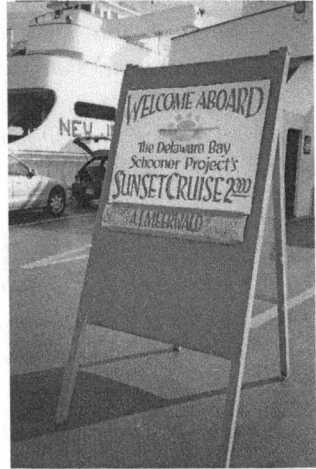

Dinner on the Cape May/ Lewes Ferry would prove to be a lucrative fundraiser. The menu was largely seafood, and many local businesses, such as Bivalve Packing, contributed the meal. *Bayshore Collection.*

give up. Week after week, volunteers continued to show up and do whatever they could. "I couldn't really even say when, but the odds turned in our favor. We got a major grant from the New Jersey Historic Trust and then one from the New Jersey Department of Transportation, and suddenly the launch was in sight."[70]

Captain Tom Carroll, retired USCG and a former chair of the New Jersey Historic Trust and the New Jersey Cultural Trust, is an innkeeper in Cape May and a longtime supporter of the *Meerwald*. In an email, Carroll recounts the story of the application for grant money to support the boat's restoration:

> *When the Historic Trust received the application for the* A.J. Meerwald, *the accompanying photos showed it sunk in the Maurice River which made it very hard to envision a finished project under sail in the Delaware Bay. As the Trust member representing the southern-most counties, I pointed out that it was a project that bay people (watermen) could really rally around as the bay had provided for them for a long time. What looks like a sunken wreck to you was a very important relic of their past and could become something to be proud of in the future. I remember that*

one of our trustees pointed out that the boat, when restored, could easily sail to another state and therefore our grants should only go to projects "anchored" to our land. That point of view almost carried the day until other members pointed out the vast sums of money we have poured into much wealthier communities to the north and agreed it was time to invest in the people and the communities in South Jersey. I sent pictures to all of them of the volunteer work teams showing up every weekend, tackling every aspect of the restoration. I was awarded with the great honor of one swing of the sledge hammer into the last spike in the hull and I have enjoyed sails aboard whenever she is docked in Cape May.[71]

Now, with funding in hand, on February 18, 1992, the *A.J.* was towed to Everett Marino's property in Bivalve, and a 275-ton crane was hired to come out, pick her out of the water and set her in a cradle on the bank. Although there was much fear that she would crack, she miraculously held together.

The first professional restoration crew was hired in March 1994, with Rick Waters as foreman for the first year. Milt Edelman was originally a member of the board of trustees but later resigned to take over as foreman. He enjoyed working on the boat and would work sixty to seventy hours per week. According to Edelman, "This was the most unusual project I ever worked on. The guys worked hard. John Tohanczyn was the most skilled of all of us." Charlie Lofft did the paperwork and the ordering. In addition to Milt and John, other shipwrights on the project included Mark Johnston, Jimmy Van Hoeck of Port Norris, Frank Blizzard and Dave DeHart. Although five or six of the men were full-time employees and there were eight or nine caulkers and riggers, it would be one and a half years until the boat was launched.

Clyde A. Phillips [Jr.] (shown here in 2000) captained the *Meerwald* during the years when his family owned the boat and had rechristened her the *Clyde A. Phillips*. He called her "the best sea boat I've ever been on." *Bayshore Collection.*

In an interview with Bob Mitchell on April 29, 2009, Clyde A. Phillips [Jr.] remembered, "That schooner has been the *A.J. Meerwald* for less time than she was the *Clyde A. Phillips*." In fact, when Meghan started an organization to put her back in commission

as a sailboat again, she called it the "Schooner Clyde A. Phillips Project."
Phillips continued, "'Schooner' refers to a sail rig, and as the *Clyde A.* (as we
called her), she was always a power boat. Dad bought her after World War II
after the Navy sold her back to the Meerwald family. We got her about 1946
or 7. I was on her papers as captain right after high school and oystered with
her. Best sea boat I've ever been on."[72]

In 1996, it would be Charlie Lofft who pushed Wren to apply for the
funds for the shipping sheds. "Charlie broke into my focus on 'today' and
suggested that I take some time for 'tomorrow' and pursue funding to build
a 'homeport' for the schooner and the organization."[73]

What did they need to do? At the start, the *Phillips* was largely a bare
hull with the rig and equipment removed. Most of the hull was intact
and contained much original material and interior woodwork, such as the
main cabin and the forecastle. The general shape and grace of the original
schooner were there, but much distortion had occurred during her years of
hard use. She showed distortion of the sheer line (the outline of the deck
from stern to bow), as well as various problems of alignment and racking.
Before any other structural work could begin, these distortions needed to
be eliminated. From the planning docs: "In general terms, the hull was in
poor condition above the waterline and in fair condition below. Dry rot had
claimed much of the deck and the upper hull."[74]

Working with the New Jersey Historic Trust and with additional funding
from the New Jersey Department of Transportation, the professional
shipwrights hired through the grants would work to preserve or restore what
could be saved and re-create other elements that might be missing but were
known to be part of the original ship.

Major components of the ship's backbone, including the keel, keelson
(fastens flooring to the keel), centerboard bed and deadwood (lower part
of the stern), were all salvageable, but much of the rest of the hull needed
considerable restoration, again following the original methods used in
building such a schooner. The centerboard had long since disappeared
and needed to be completely reconstructed. These hull components were
to be a mix of long-leaf yellow pine, white oak and yellow pine. While
some of these woods were locally available, much had to be brought in
from North Carolina or other areas. The deck underwent considerable
rebuilding of cedar planking, with one starboard quarter section of the
bulwarks remaining original.

"Two hippies from New England made the masts," Edelman remembers.
The spars were of Douglas fir from the West Coast and were purchased

The ship had been painted green sometime during her days as a clammer, and when she was finally readied for restoration, it was found dry rot had claimed much of the deck and upper hull. She is shown here in the summer of 1994. *Courtesy of the photographer Michael J. Chiarappa.*

from Jim Elk, a spar builder from Bar Harbor, Maine. The ship began to take back its original shape. The masts—actually trees—were made to dimension in Port Norris by Jim Elk and a helper, Dave Brown. Elk rounded out a massive length of Douglas fir by hand to create the seventy-foot-tall masts. The effort took about two weeks, according to Lofft.

Measurement for the sails came from the sails of the schooner *Sheppard Campbell*, which were donated. The sailmaker came from northeast Pennsylvania, material for the sails came from Bridgeton and the blocks were made in Lunenburg, Nova Scotia.

As the work progressed, discoveries of more work needed occurred on a regular basis. Inspections were held by the United States Coast Guard Marine Safety Office from Philadelphia, and approvals were given for work accomplished, as well as for the plans as they adapted to the actuality of the *Meerwald*'s poor condition. Again, according to Lofft, a total of two hundred planks were replaced in the framing of the ship.

Inside the ship, a good percentage of the forepeak cabin, containing berths for eight hands, was able to be saved. Mike Chiarappa led a field

One on-shore activity for local students is the Kids About the Bay. Fifth graders from Cumberland County schools spend the day on the docks and sheds learning about the environment and the history of the Delaware Bay. *Bayshore Collection, gift of the photographer Michael Schuelke, 2018.*

On the educational sail, students have an opportunity to help raise the *Meerwald*'s sails. *Bayshore Collection.*

The crew from 2013. Now you know what "standing out on the chains" means. Fourth from left is Jesse Briggs, who captained the ship for twenty years, with his young son Delbay sitting in the bow. *Bayshore Collection.*

The *William Veale*, an old-style schooner, is shown at left with a top-sail and clipper bow. The *C.M. Riggin* in full sail is bald-headed and has the new spoon bow. *Bayshore Collection, photographer Graham L. Schofield.*

Francis and Edna Meerwald's Wonderland of Lights, 1977. Their Christmas display of eighteen thousand lights was well known. It was at the old Meerwald homestead in South Dennis, also home to thirty thousand chickens. *Courtesy of Teri L. Watson.*

The work site at Marino's for the restoration of the *Meerwald*. *Bayshore Collection.*

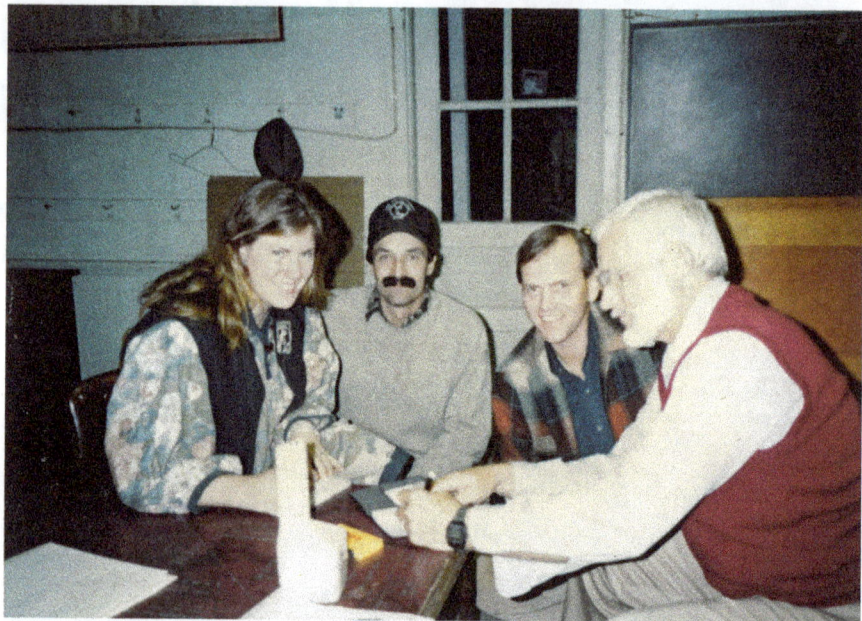

Clyde A. Phillips [Jr.] (*far right*) signs up for the first membership of the Schooner Project on November 1, 1988. From the left are Meghan Wren, Greg Honachefsky and John Gandy. *Bayshore Collection, courtesy of the photographer J.W. Walton Jr.*

George Schupp looking pleased with the restoration so far. *Bayshore Collection.*

The groundbreaking ceremony for the restoration of the shipping sheds on May 12, 2008. *Bayshore Collection.*

The shipping sheds restoration is seen here on January 1, 2009. The ribbon cutting is twenty months away. *Bayshore Collection.*

A unique view of the restoration from the interior of the ship. *Bayshore Collection.*

The shaping of the masts—from round to square to octagon to sixteen-sided to thirty-two-sided and back to round again. *Bayshore Collection.*

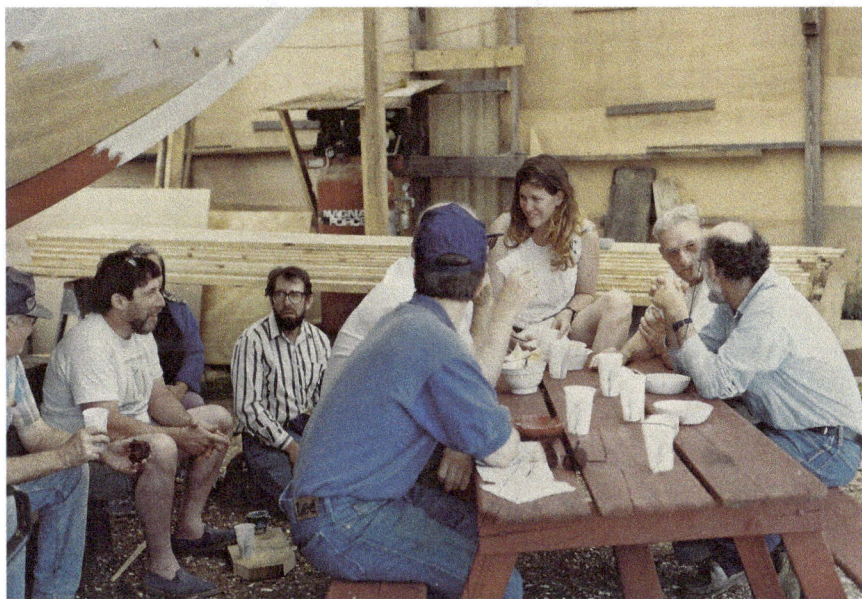

Meghan having lunch with volunteers and workers. To her right in the white T-shirt is Milt Edelman, the foreman. *Bayshore Collection.*

The first launching, minus sails, shows she is able to float. *Bayshore Collection.*

Taking lines or measuring to create a plan. *Courtesy of the photographer Michael Chiarappa.*

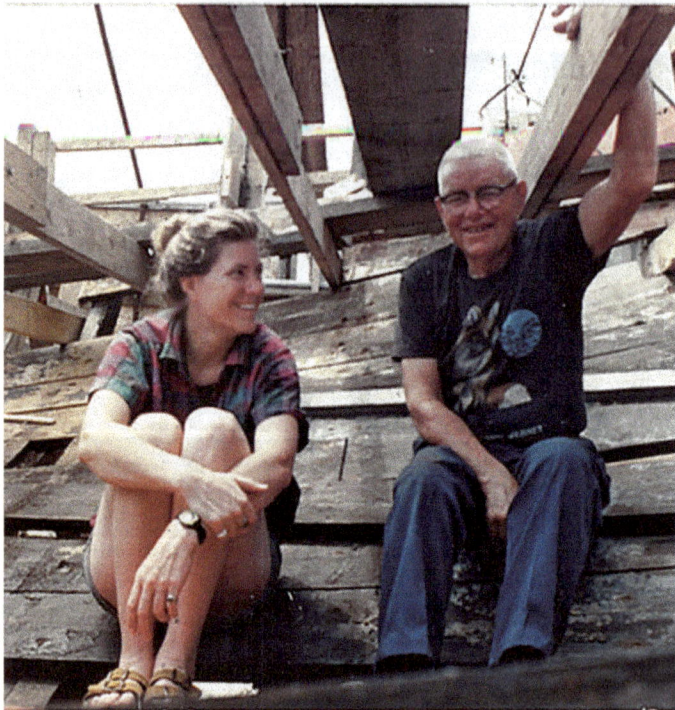

Mort Hughes and Meghan Wren taking a break in the summer of 1994. *Bayshore Collection.*

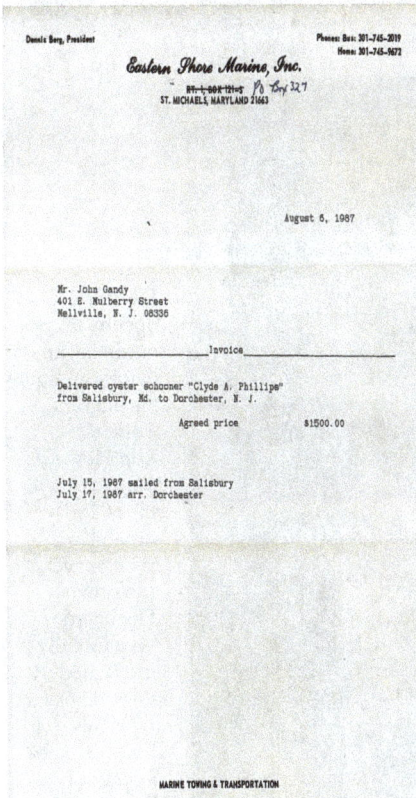

Eastern Shore Marine, Inc.

Dennis Berg, President

Phones: Bus: 301-745-2019
Home: 301-745-9672

Rt. 1, BOX 121-5 PO Box 327
ST. MICHAELS, MARYLAND 21663

August 6, 1987

Mr. John Gandy
401 E. Mulberry Street
Mellville, N. J. 08336

_____ Invoice _____

Delivered oyster schooner "Clyde A. Phillips"
from Salisbury, Md. to Dorchester, N. J.

Agreed price $1500.00

July 15, 1987 sailed from Salisbury
July 17, 1987 arr. Dorchester

MARINE TOWING & TRANSPORTATION

Above: Captain Larry Hickman and his crew: Billy Fiswell Jr., Eric Jupin, Fast Ed Givens, Pat Shaver and Larry Catlett Sr. on the *John C. Peterson*, dredging and hand-culling oysters at the Ship John Lighthouse, September 20, 2016. *Courtesy of the photographer Rachel Cobb Photography & Design.*

Left: The cost of bringing the schooner from Salisbury to Dorchester was $1,500. *Courtesy of John Gandy.*

An aerial shot of the work site showing the ship already pretty far along toward restoration. Photos from above were taken using a kite (pre-drone days). *Bayshore Collection, gift of the photographer Steve Eisenhauer.*

Directing a documentary on the awful living conditions for migrant workers, Ron Howard came to town with Cloris Leachman, Sissy Spacek and others. The actors were friendly and signed autographs for the locals. *Port Norris Historical Society, courtesy of Faye Hickman.*

Maurice River

The wetlands or marshes along the banks of the Delaware are an important part of our ecosystem. In a natural state, wetlands build up, unless eroded, tampered by humans or subject to sea level rise. Pictured here is the historic Burcham Farmhouse, circa 1860, the last remaining diked farm on the Maurice River. Lack of natural accretion due to farming leaves the former wetland lower than the level of the river. A system of ditches and sluice gates allows the farm fields to be drained. *Courtesy of CU Maurice River.*

An early supporter of the Schooner Project, Al Huber was instrumental in particular in fundraising. He sported a license plate that shows his interest in the oyster industry. *Bayshore Collection.*

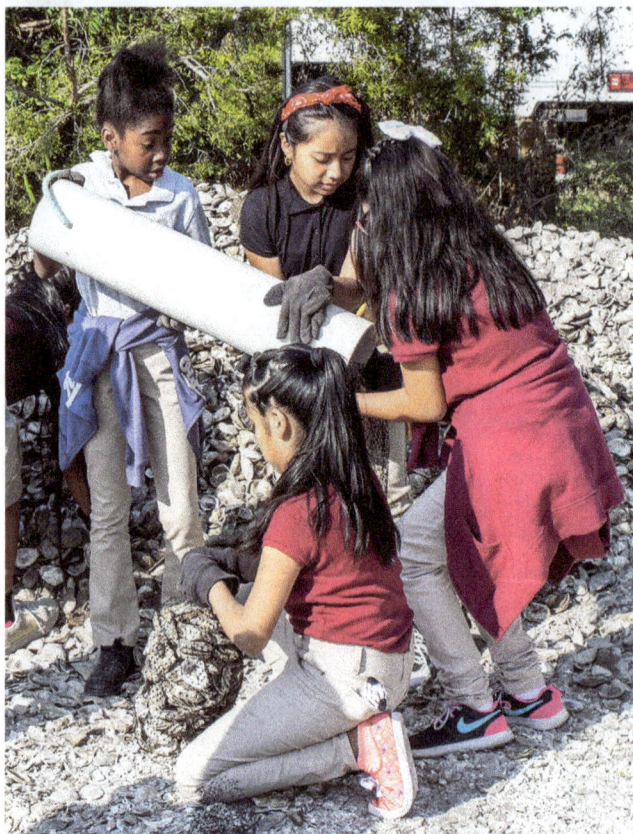

Left: Kids shell bagging during Kids About the Bay, 2019. They are hauling bags of oyster shells to aid in the restoration of the oyster beds. *Bayshore Collection, gift of the photographer Michael Schuelke.*

Below: Oyster roast fundraiser, 2019. Pat Shaver and Tony Klock handle oysters straight off the grill. *Bayshore Collection, gift of the photographer Seth Beaumont.*

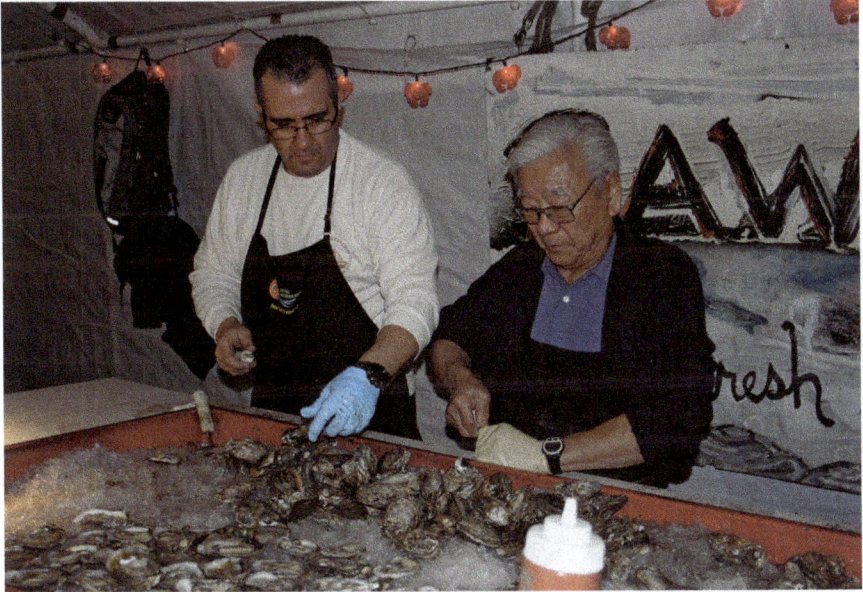

Above: Freshly shucked oysters are in demand at Second Fridays on the piers. Volunteers Mike Fardone and Roy Kaneshiki work to meet the demand. *Bayshore Collection.*

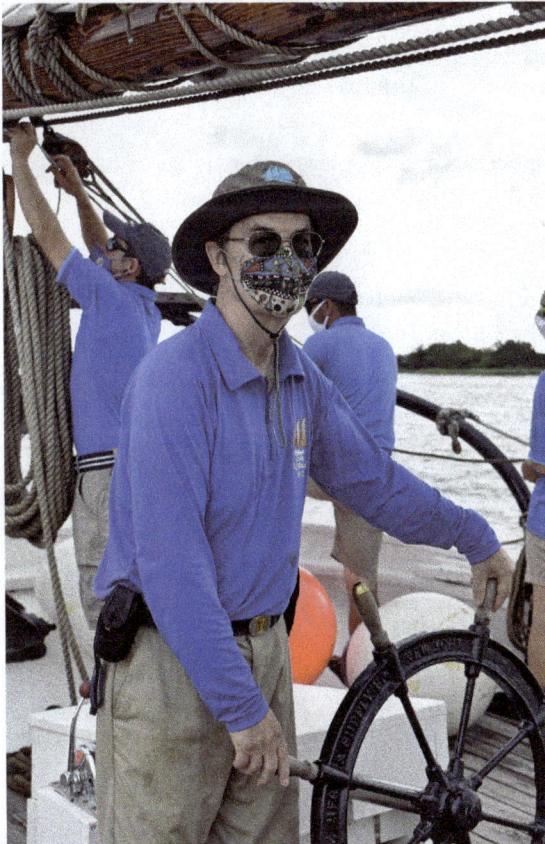

Left: Volunteers are crucial to the many functions of the Bayshore Center. Here, Tom Nichols lends a hand at the helm. *Bayshore Collection.*

Coauthor Rachel Dolhanczyk (*center*) with Gladys Meerwald Brewer, Gus and Edna's daughter, and her daughter Cynthia Brewer Sano. Mrs. Brewer's husband, Robert Brewer, is to the far left, and BCB's executive director, Brian Keenan, is to the far right. November 2018. *Bayshore Collection.*

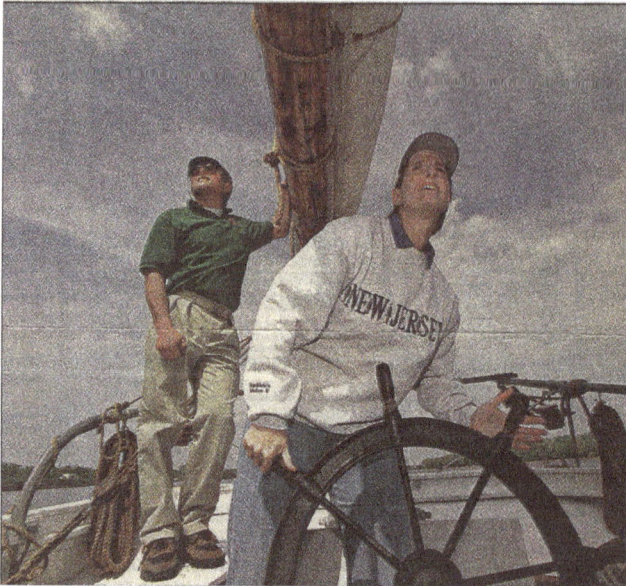

Governor Christie Todd Whitman takes the helm under the supervision of Mitch Brodkin, one of the *Meerwald*'s captains, during the Official Tall Ship of New Jersey designation. *From the* Press *of Atlantic City, New Jersey, April 22, 1998.*

Coauthor McCart teaching the oyster station on board, 2008. *Courtesy of C. McCart, photograph by Frank McCart.*

Meerwald under sail in Baltimore, Maryland. *Courtesy of C. McCart, photograph by Frank McCart.*

The *A.J. Meerwald* sailing toward the sunset on the Delaware Bay, Cape May. *Bayshore Collection, gift of the photographer Eric Haugen, 2007.*

The deck needed nearly complete rebuilding, although one section starboard remained original. The wood needed to work on the boat was found in various parts of the Eastern Seaboard states. Here Meghan Wren, the head of the Schooner Project, is shown caulking. *Bayshore Collection.*

school in maritime preservation for his students from the graduate program in American and public history at Rutgers University–Camden. Using research and documentation, the students worked to preserve the aft cabin, which had been removed from the hull. In the aft cabin, four berths are available for captain and mate, and the working machinery of the boat is housed here, such as the modern technology used to sail the ship now, charts and access to the engine room. While the original hold would have been empty, it now houses crew, galley, head and gear.

The *Meerwald* was originally built with a one-hundred-horsepower standard diesel engine but was known to carry a 6-71 Gray Marine diesel engine at several points in her career. During the restoration, a similar 6-71 diesel engine was installed. The schooner rig had of course been removed many years prior but was reconstructed using historic photographs as a guide and using parts of old rigs from similar local vessels and the memories of the old-timers who had sailed the oyster boats.

As to her exterior appearance, it has long been traditional for the Delaware Bay schooners to be painted white with three stripes—yellow, blue and red—

Left: Mike Chiarappa not only volunteered on the project (shown here labeling the planks) but brought a group of student interns to help as well. *Courtesy of Michael J. Chiarappa.*

Below: Meghan Wren is shown ready for the launch. The *Meerwald* once again sports the traditional white paint with three stripes—yellow, blue and red—highlighting the graceful lines of the schooner. *Bayshore Collection.*

to highlight the sweeping lines of the ship. The stripes were determined from a painting by Florence Meerwald shared by Frank Unkle, a grandson of William and Florence. In the painting, she also sported two gold balls atop each of her masts, so these were replaced as well.

About 10 percent of the original vessel is extant. The *A.J. Meerwald* is considered to be restored, not rebuilt, since repairs and replacements added during the restoration were carefully chosen to be consistent with the methods and materials used in the original schooner. Since the oyster fleet schooners have continued to be repaired and maintained by the Dorchester shipyard and other nearby yards, the needs were readily known. It is even possible that some of the replacement wood may have been cut from the same stands of wood used in the 1920s.

A year and a half after the haul-out and seven after the origination of the project, the *Meerwald* was relaunched. A good-size crowd attended. A band played, the sun shone and "people jockeyed for positions as Players; no one seemed content to be just an onlooker—everyone had helped make it happen—even the old timers who drove by once in a while to heckle."[75] On September 12, 1995, Wren christened the ship, smashing the traditional bottle of champagne over her bow. Waters, Edelman, Hughes and Van Hoeck lowered the boat into the water. The *A.J. Meerwald* finally sailed once more. She would begin offering educational sails as of May 1996 with Mark Crutcher as the first captain. The work of maintaining that restoration continues.

The *J. Roberts Bateman* escorted the *Meerwald* back to Dorchester, where she would be rigged and outfitted. After a test raising of the sails, the *Meerwald* sailed first up the river to be sure she would pass coast guard inspection. Her first formal sail was to Penns Landing in Philadelphia, where the coast guard conducted the needed inspections, and she was certified to sail with forty-nine passengers and crew on April 18, 1996.[76]

In spite of finding problems as the restoration progressed, the completion of the work was only one month off the original estimate. Though the restoration process had begun in March 1994, by 1996, the *Meerwald* was taking passengers. She had been approved in just over two years.

These years proved to be extremely busy and productive. The Bayshore Center opened the Maritime Traditions of the Delaware Bay Museum at its headquarters on Main Street in Port Norris. The South Jersey Traditional Small Craft Association built a replica yawl boat for the *A.J. Meerwald* led by Ron Heron, foreman; Will Hutton; Bob Scheetz; George Loos; Chuck Pritchard; and Dom Beningo.

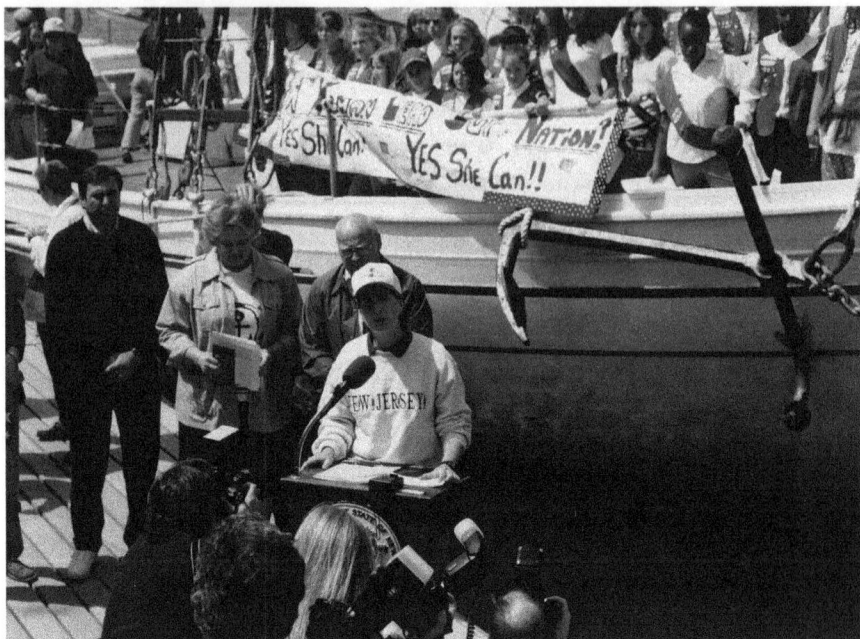

A letter-writing campaign helped to persuade the state assembly and then-governor Christie Todd Whitman to name the *Meerwald* New Jersey's Official Tall Ship in April 1998. The designation of "tall ship" happily was accompanied by $95,000 in state funds. Governor Whitman is at the mic with legislators Diane Allen and Nick Asselta to her right. *Bayshore Collection.*

In 1997, a letter campaign instigated by the Bayshore Center began to importune the legislature to name the *Meerwald* New Jersey's "Official Tall Ship." Support came from all areas. The Atlantic County freeholder board adopted a resolution to honor the ship, and articles appeared in the *Courier-Post*, the *Atlantic City Press* and the *Philadelphia Inquirer*. Letters of endorsement came from J.F. Grassle, director of the Institute of Marine and Coastal Sciences; the president of Cumberland County College; and John Maier, the executive director of the South Jersey Port Corporation.

Perhaps most persuasive and certainly most poignant were the letters submitted to the New Jersey State Assembly. Fifth grader Jessica Cobb wrote, "Other states will see the schooner carrying the flag and they will not just say, 'Look at that boat!' but they will also say, 'Look at that New Jersey flag!'…If the *A.J. Meerwald* becomes our state's tall ship, it will be New Jersey's dignity and it will carry the flag proudly."[77]

Bill A750/S485 was announced, sponsored by Assemblymen Asselta and Gibson of the First District and Assemblymen Collins and Stuhltrager of

Governor Christie Todd Whitman takes a hand at the helm under the supervision of Mitch Brodkin, one of the captains for the *A.J. Meerwald*. *From the* Press *of Atlantic City, New Jersey, April 22, 1998.*

the Third. In the Senate, Cafiero and Zane of the First District were co-sponsors with Diane Allen of Burlington County.

Flyers were sent to both houses urging a yes vote. After a successful vote, the Bayshore Center asked the public to write to Governor Whitman to ensure her signature. The April 22 *Atlantic City Press* announced Whitman's signature approving the bill into law. "The refurbished oyster schooner, the *A.J. Meerwald*, has joined the ranks of the violet, Eastern Goldfinch and honey bee in being official symbols of New Jersey." Following the bill signing ceremony, Whitman boarded the ship for an hour-long cruise, during which Captain Mitch Brodkin gave her a chance to man the helm.

Whitman noted that the *A.J. Meerwald* is a reminder of a significant chapter in New Jersey's history. "A time when sailing vessels like the *Meerwald* were the backbone of this region's economy and culture,' she said."[78] The designation was not just symbolic but also came with $95,000 in state funds to help maintain and operate the ship.

"There is kind of a language happening here when we talk about these boat parts that only we might understand...and a true love for the beauty of what we are preserving," concedes Karl Kramer, sixty-five, of Alloway Township, Salem County, who is among the volunteers who braved a particularly cold and windy day recently to work on the boat's keel. Kramer says he's motivated to brave the elements for hours to work on the boat—and volunteer as a deckhand on the *Meerwald* during the summer—because of the chance to get his hands on history instead of just reading about it in a book.[79]

In Meghan Wren's words:

> *I think the most important thing that has allowed the project to continue is the outpouring of support from so many different people. It's a community-based sort of groundswell from individuals becoming a larger entity—the pride and the whole region and the personal character of the whole Delaware Bay area, that's embodied in this vessel.*[80]

> *Today, the* A.J. Meerwald *sails as New Jersey's Official Tall Ship. She is one of the few tall ships—only three—to be restored rather than replicated. The moral to the story is that great things can be accomplished little by little with perseverance and teamwork. If the* Meerwald *can sail again, the Delaware Bay can again be a thriving ecosystem and lifeblood of the Bayshore community....Most things aren't as overwhelming as they may seem at first glance—the* A.J. Meerwald *wasn't rebuilt in a day.*[81]

Chapter 4

OYSTERS

It was a nice time because even though it was a rough environment, the community did stick together, everyone knew everyone, the community helped raise you as a child and there was respect for the other people. No delinquency as I recall it, ever, there were no race problems.... We went to school with Caucasian people. We played together, and that's the way it was from the '40s, '50s and '60s when I grew up.... It was really kind of a utopian society that I grew up in. It was kind of a melting pot that worked for the good of an industry, which was the oyster.
—Lionel Hickman interview, 2005

*T*he Greeks built a temple for the oysters. Rome burned while Nero slurped, and Richard III declared, "My kingdom for an oyster!"
Well, maybe not quite, but there is no question of the oyster's importance. Shots have been fired, millionaires have been made and ships have been confiscated over oysters. The oyster has been an extremely popular and lucrative culinary choice for most of man's history. In the Delaware Bay area, the rise and fall of the oyster industry was responsible for the growth and then the dissipation of towns and shantytowns and generated a culture and way of life that now struggles to stay afoot.

Zoologists believe that oysters first appeared in the Triassic period along with those popular fellows the dinosaurs. Fossils have shown that the species dates as far back as two hundred million years ago. Tales abound of paleontologists' fantastic finds of large layers of fossilized oyster shells in shallow waters throughout America and Europe. "Near a small town called Stetten in Austria, a huge field of fossils was discovered in 2005, with some monstrous 3 foot long shells unearthed."[82] The town, far from the sea, now has a museum exhibit dedicated to the oyster.

In spite of the oyster's rock-hard surface and, to some, unappetizing appearance once opened, Stone Age man was apparently convinced to try eating oysters, perhaps by watching the gulls drop the mollusk onto rocks to break it open or watching the intrepid otter use a flat rock to break it open. Archaeologists have found oyster shells showing traces of scorch marks, indicating that early man may also have heated the oyster a bit to pop open the shells.[83]

While nomadic or semi-nomadic early man relished trekking to the shore in the warm weather to enjoy the many types of seafood available, the oyster would have been particularly popular due to the ease of finding this food. Once spawned, the oyster conveniently clings to the nearby shells and becomes sessile, meaning it never moves again. A convenient meal, readily available at the same spot as last season! However, the Greeks were the ones to first actually cultivate the oyster.

First Cultivation

It is said that Greek fishermen first noticed that oyster babies were noted to grow frequently on broken pottery shards discarded in coastal waters. They then collected these oyster babies and transplanted them for commercial use. The cultivation method is to first collect suitable underpinnings, called cultch, and then spread this material in a chosen shallow water area, a process called shelling. The spat are then moved to another watery location to continue to grow to marketable size. This is the method of modern oyster cultivation worldwide.

According to various sources, it wasn't Nero but the Roman emperor Vitellius who supposedly managed to imbibe one thousand oysters at one dinner. Roman dignitaries considered the oyster a must-have for any important occasion, to the extent that they eventually began to wipe out the Mediterranean beds, even posting guards to keep those remaining from being poached. Fortunately for them, they conquered large areas of the European coastline and then were able to raid these beds in turn. Packed in snow, they carted them home to Rome. These difficulties led the Romans to work on cultivation of the mollusks as well.

Oysters are sessile, meaning they attach themselves as spat, or babies, to discarded shells or other hard surfaces and then never move again. *Courtesy of Cumberland County Historical Society, photographer Harvey Porch.*

Oysters continued to be harvested throughout medieval times into the present by being cultivated in a limited sense, but eventually, the oyster beds in Europe and Britain were severely overfished, and prices began to rise. It would not be until the modern era that man would learn the two crucial lessons to be discussed later in this chapter about conserving oysters.

Oysters are not just a food source. In past centuries, shells were used as money, utensils or decorations. Oyster shells have been used as paving, ground into calcium carbonate to add to cement or to treat wastewater. Crushed oyster shells are used as an animal and poultry feed or as mulch in gardens, improving soil health.

Most importantly, oysters are filter feeders. They each process fifty gallons of water per day, removing algae, plankton and other particles that impact the clarity of water. Their reefs also contribute to the environment by creating stability in the water, reducing soil erosion and flooding. Their presence is also beneficial to many other species of sea plants and animals. "When shellfish are planted and are able to reproduce and broadcast their larvae, that has the direct impact of increasing different fish populations, as well as improving waters so that more shellfish can survive," says David

Bushek. He's director of the Rutgers University Haskin Shellfish Research Laboratory in New Jersey. "Also, [oyster reef] habitat is used by other organisms as a nursery or place to forage, which increases those populations, including fish that [humans] go after."[84]

How the Oyster Got to Be King

Port Norris and Bivalve are villages located on the Maurice River just as it flows into the Delaware Bay. The Delaware Bay is part of the estuary that runs from Artificial Island near Handcocks Bridge in the north and down to Cape May in the south. This is an important tidal waterway for many reasons; it has facilitated travel through the region for two centuries, and its broad variety of wildlife and wetlands has provided a living, an industry and a market for oysters as well as other seafood.

Oysters like a briny mix of fresh and salt water, as is found in the Delaware Bay. The local natives, the Lenni-Lenape, who summered at the shore just as we do today, found the oysters at low tide, and as the colonists came to the area, they learned this was a reliable food source. Beyond nutrition, the oyster shells were burned for mortar or were used as fertilizer or roadbeds.[85]

As early as 1719, New Jersey enacted laws to limit the use of the oyster beds by those not from the state and limited the number of boats oystering. In the next century, shortages were noticed in northern beds, and cultivation became common. In 1846, New Jersey passed a law closing oyster beds in the summer. The state retained ownership of the oyster beds and leased the sections to the oystermen. Further laws would be enacted between 1860 and 1995.

Oysters grew and reproduced naturally in the upper seed beds of the Maurice River Cove, where the salinity is lowest, but oystermen transported them down the bay in the spring, where the water has higher salinity and is warmer, enabling the oysters to grow fat and tasty for the harvest. While oysters in the Delaware Bay were originally taken from the shallows using tongs and rakes, the introduction of the oyster dredge—a rake with a chain basket—led to increased harvest. Tonging does continue on a more limited basis.

The schooners pulled a dredge behind them, and the catch was directly harvested onto the boat's shallow deck. From the schooners, the catch was loaded into floats along the banks of the river, where they fattened and cleaned for a day or two. They were then shoveled from the float into scows

While we are most familiar with oysters being raked from the water bed, some individuals use tongs (long versions of our kitchen utensil) to scoop up the oysters. *Courtesy of Cumberland County Historical Society, photographer Harvey Porch.*

(flat-bottomed boats). The oysters were culled for size, counted into bushel baskets and then poured into sacks or barrels, which were wheeled from the dock up to the boxcars.

During the nineteenth century, boats typically had a five-man crew who often owned shares in the boat. The work was difficult. The workday stretched from dawn to sunset, and winter work was often hampered by ice. Oystermen spent only their Sundays on shore; they rode the Saturday afternoon train from Port Norris to home and back again on Monday morning. At the time, the average earnings for those in the industry was eighty to one hundred dollars per month. Oysters still shipped in the shell, and 95 percent of the catch at that time went to Philadelphia via water.[86]

Port Norris and the small village of Bivalve—named after its main product, two-sided, hinged shell mollusks—would grow extensively during the nineteenth century. The coming of the railroads was responsible for much of that growth. Originally, oysters were forwarded to Philadelphia in small sailboats, a trip that took a week. Steam-propelled boats ran between Bivalve and New York and Philadelphia by 1860, but they proved not to pay.[87]

Then, Ebenezer Wescott organized the Bridgeton and Port Norris Railroad in March 1866 for the sole purpose of taking advantage of money to be made from the oyster trade. Its main founders and subscribers were merchants from Fairfield Township, Downe Township and other local areas. The line ran from Bridgeton to Fairton and Cedarville and eventually to Port Norris. The first trains proved a failure at first, as the roadbeds had been poorly designed, causing mudslides that impeded the engine's progress, but by the summer of 1873, the train was running for both passengers and freight. Passengers consisted of workers in the oyster industry, and the freight

A group of workers is shown with bags and baskets of oysters in the era prior to the oysters being shucked before shipping. Luther Bateman is shown on the right. *Courtesy of Cumberland County Historical Society, photographer Harvey Porch.*

was largely oysters. However, the company did not do well, partly as the section of rail between Mauricetown and Port Norris was so low it actually settled into the marsh and came under water.

After a bankruptcy, the Bridgeton line reorganized as the Cumberland and Maurice River Railroad and made repairs. It began to ship fourteen to twenty carloads of freight daily, while the population of Port Norris and Bivalve grew steadily.[88]

Another factor in the growth of the area was, of course, refrigeration, originally achieved by creating commercial ice and later transitioning to refrigeration as we know it. A major force in the increase in business was the refrigerated railroad car. In 1867, a J.B. Sutherland of Detroit created an insulated railroad car with ice bunkers at either end, ensuring that oysters could be safely transported farther distances and at a low cost. Oysters soon became the most important fishery product in the United

Oyster accessories became popular along with the bivalve. Shown is a very collectible oyster plate used to serve them on the half shell or raw. *Bayshore Collection, gift of Meredith Rapp.*

States. By 1880, 2.4 million bushels were being harvested, and oysters were a multimillion-dollar industry.

Oysters at the time were inexpensive. They are also nutritious and can be prepared in numerous ways, from simply serving them raw to making pies, stews, stuffings or any other way you can imagine. And nineteenth-century Americans had plenty of imagination. Cookbooks from that time generally include many recipes for the mollusk. At a local dinner for an industry anniversary in 1907, a surviving menu includes oysters in the shell as a first course, followed by oyster patties as a second course, and after a main course of turkey with oyster stuffing, broiled oysters were served along with rolls and crackers. Three-pronged oyster forks became a necessity at dinner parties, and a popular collectible is found in the elaborately decorated porcelain oyster plates with their just-right-sized indentations to hold the oyster safely.

THE TOWN OF PORT NORRIS AND ITS VILLAGE, BIVALVE

Port Norris was founded in 1738 as the town of Dallas Ferry, named after its first resident. The land there was eventually purchased by Joseph Coffee, who renamed the town after his son, Norris. Oysters were shipped to Philadelphia on sloops until the development of the schooner, which was larger and more suited to the oyster trade.

In the 1830s, the town of Port Norris had only eight buildings, and its main industry was to ship wood and lumber. Once the railroad came to the Maurice River, the population jumped to over 800, and eventually, by the end of the nineteenth century, 1,800 souls called Port Norris home. Bivalve, the section directly on the water, became the major shipping point for Delaware Bay oysters to Philadelphia and beyond.

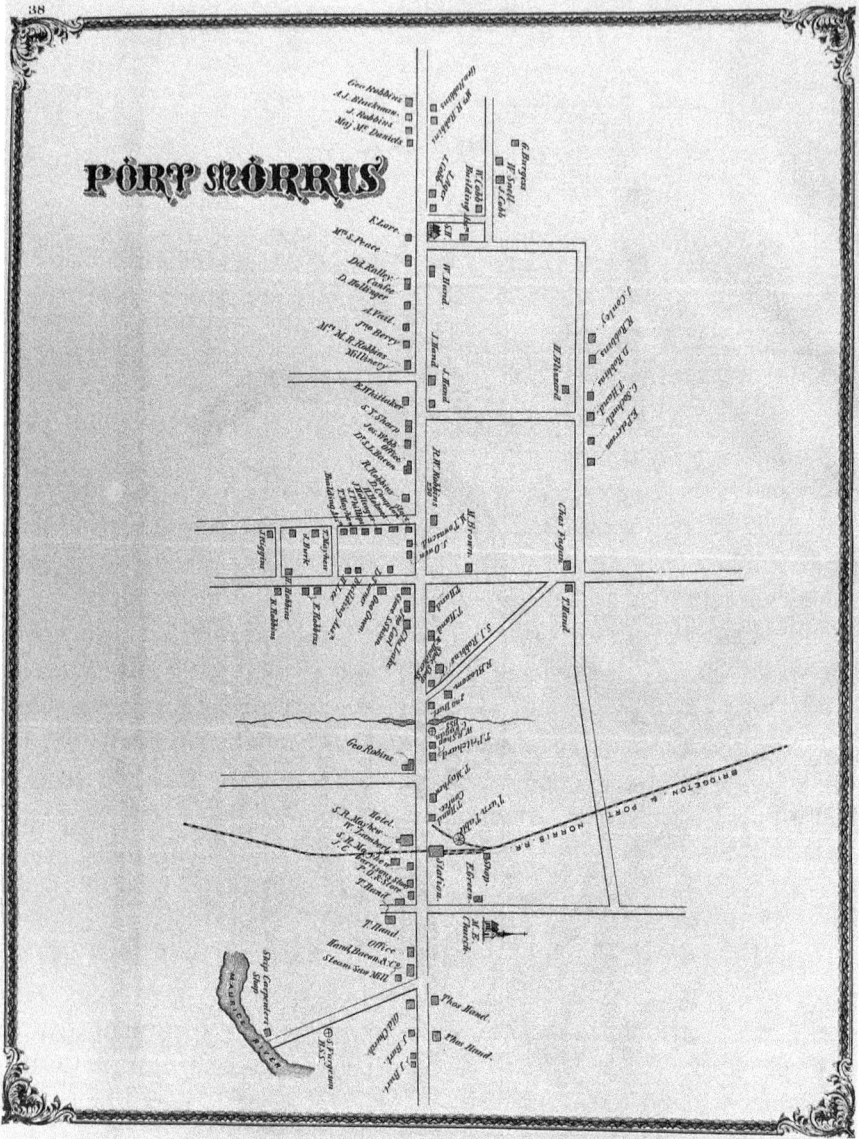

Above: A map of Port Norris showing the growth of the town as oysters became a growing industry. *D.F. Stewart*, New Historical Atlas of Cumberland County, New Jersey, Illustrated *(1876), Bayshore Collection, gift of Scott Eves.*

Opposite: A group of men packing oysters at Bivalve, circa 1909, at the oyster sheds. *Bayshore Collection, gift of Bill Biggs.*

The Central Railroad of New Jersey would take over the Cumberland and Maurice River Railroad. Pennsylvania Railroad built the West Jersey line directly across the river from Bivalve, then called Long Reach, in 1887. The West Jersey Railroad also operated a ferry between Bivalve and Maurice River. Between the two stations, over eighty rail cars of oysters were shipped per day. The railroad connected Bivalve with Philadelphia and New York and allowed for the popular oysters to be delivered to those cities within a day. By the early twentieth century, Maurice River Cove oysters, the country's number-one fishery product, were served from Baltimore to New York and west as far as Chicago, Denver and San Francisco.

In 1883, Thomas Cushing and Charles Shephard wrote in their history the following account:

> *Oysters are put up in strong coarse sacks holding 750 prime mollusks or 100 or more cullings. The average shipment by rail is 90 car loads a week, about 20,000 oysters to the car. It is an immense trade with oysters of excellent quality and a constantly increasing demand. Consequently, the town of Port Norris is rapidly growing with new and "handsome" homes being built. A school house, with a hall and bell was completed in 1882. Hand, Robbins & Burt have a steam saw-mill there along with a shipyard for the repair of boats owned by Thomas Hand. Shops exist to provide all types of instruments needed for the industry. By the census of 1880, the population of Port Norris was 885, but now has increased to 1,000.*[89]

By 1880, the population of Port Norris had increased beyond one thousand persons, and the town even boasted a hotel. *Bayshore Collection, gift of Bill Biggs.*

By the early 1900s, southern New Jersey was the largest oyster-producing region in the nation, with a crop of approximately 3,600,000 bushels.[90] The town of Port Norris and the village of Bivalve grew accordingly. There were several eateries in Bivalve, including Mrs. E. Meredith's Restaurant, which specialized (of course) in dishes of oysters; the G.W. Pasley's Restaurant, selling oysters and ice cream; and the Blizzard Restaurant. In Port Norris, Garrison's Restaurant advertised as "an old bed newly stuck up." Some of the local recipes that were available in the Port Norris restaurants besides oyster stew included snapper soup, muskrat potpie and weakfish roe.[91]

Other businesses also grew along with the shellfish, some of them finding other uses for the products. Shell-grinding plants sold shells for road-making material or as grit for poultry feed and fertilizer. Some commerce appeared built around servicing the boats, including boat yards such as that at Dorchester and the sail loft at Bivalve owned by Robert DuBois and E.B. Cobb. Lewis Shropshire of Mauricetown manufactured winders for use on the dredge boats. Trolley service also developed between Port Norris and Bridgeton.[92]

The established gentlemen of the town belonged to fraternal organizations such as the Order of Red Men and the Masons. The Junior Order of American Mechanics provided disability insurance and death benefits for

A trolley ran through Port Norris as well, leading to Bridgeton and Millville. *Bayshore Collection, gift of Bill Biggs.*

young white men associated with the oyster industry. Baseball had its Oyster League in Port Norris, and there were minstrel shows and a theater showing silent movies and weekly dances. The town boasted its own newspaper, the *Advisor Press*, and the Davis Hotel welcomed visitors. Milton Sheppard owned the Sea Shell Restaurant, and the town boasted a telephone exchange, a beauty parlor and three doctors.

In Bivalve at that time, there was a bake shop, two clothing stores and a funeral parlor. Two yard goods stores sold fabric and notions, and Dan Bateman had a grocery store, as did High and Thurston. An ice cream parlor existed on the wharf, as well as a barbershop.[93]

Rita Moonsammy describes the churches—Baptist and Presbyterian— and the social life of the upper class of the town families in her dissertation on the schooner era. The Robbins family, for one, settled in an area of Port Norris that would become known as Robbinsville. Here, the most prosperous of the families lived in their large Victorian-style homes. Perhaps giving rise to the legend of the "millionaires of Port Norris," the Robbins family by 1903 owned at least nine oyster boats and leased over 1,500 acres of oyster beds.

Between 1860 and the early 1900s, Bivalve was an industrious community that lived by the tides of the oyster. With the exception of Christmas, all

Left: The Main Street of Port Norris, showing rows of substantial homes. *Bayshore Collection, gift of Bill Biggs.*

Below: The DuBois Sail Loft was one of many complementary businesses that supported the oyster industry at Bivalve. *Courtesy of Cumberland County Historical Society, photographer Harvey Porch.*

holidays in Bivalve were celebrated on Sundays because that's when Bivalve's oystermen were home.[94]

In an interview for the Citizens United Maurice River Reaches Project, Warrington Hollinger talked about the introduction of wild ponies to the Port Norris area. "At one time, we had five hundred Chincoteague ponies down there," Hollinger said. "And we had a half-mile racetrack there." Hollinger said that the racetrack was as popular as Woodstown's Cowtown Rodeo is today. Old-timers also reminisce about the little racetrack that kept the buzz in Port Norris after working hours. This was the life when the region was known as the "Oyster Capital of the World."[95]

"We used to have a big celebration there once a year," Hollinger recalled. He said that winnings were paid out in silver dollars. This was a lively era in the history of Port Norris, and the Hollinger family played an important role in the community. In addition to their business holdings, they operated the rodeo and provided the impetus for community celebrations.

Hollinger said that his uncle brought the ponies to Port Norris. "My uncle went down to Chincoteague and bought five hundred ponies. Ponies ran all over that meadow for a number of years," he said. That was back in the mid-1930s. Hollinger said that some of the ponies stayed close to the barns on the property, but most ran loose on the meadow. That era ended when some kind of disease was transmitted through the grasses of the meadows. "It wiped practically all of them out," Hollinger said.[96]

Oyster Wars

But not all of this development went smoothly. Of the many edible seafoods the oceans and bays provide, only the oyster is farmed. At first, the industry was a first-come, first-served type of process, with those with the most money and the most boats pulling in the largest catch and making the most money.

This led to conflicts and lawsuits. In 1820, New Jersey passed legislation creating a closed season for gathering oysters, whether raking or dredging, and also made it illegal for anyone but a New Jersey resident to take oysters from the state's waters. On May 15, 1821, three boats from Philadelphia—including the *Hiram*, a sloop—were seen dredging for oysters in New Jersey waters. The crew of the Leesburg, New Jersey schooner the *Independence* seized all three boats and sold the *Hiram*. A lawsuit was brought.[97]

The *Hiram*'s lawyer claimed the Jersey boat and crew were excessively aggressive, raising the United States flag and shouting orders to fire, although they never actually did so. The men from the *Hiram* reported seeing arms and boarding pikes aboard the schooner. And when the *Independence* returned to Leesburg, she was greeted enthusiastically, as if having won a battle. However, the defense contended they had no real arms to speak of but only a swivel, a small mounted cannon, described as "a nasty, noisy, ugly disagreeable thing."

The main crux of the lawsuit, however, was whether New Jersey had the right to restrict by whom, when and where oystering would take place in its waters. In the end, the judge determined that the Maurice River Cove where the boat had been captured was in New Jersey's jurisdiction and subject to its laws. Since the *Hiram* was also operating out of season, the *Independence* and its owner were acquitted easily. Interestingly, the other two boat owners were dismissed of charges, largely because they were poor, while the *Hiram* was owned by a wealthy Philadelphia lawyer. He and his boat were treated more harshly because he was felt to be easily able to afford the loss of the catch.

Conflicts continued over the rights to oyster beds, inflamed to some extent by a decline in the production of natural oysters. By the late 1880s, riparian grants to provide private property of underwater land were common. Six miles of the bayshore had been allotted to oystermen who paid for these rights. In 1886, these included Luther Bateman, James G. Gandy and the Bradfords.[98]

Further dissent arose as some claimed it gave an unfair advantage to those few who could afford to purchase the grants. In April 1884, vessels began dredging on a private grant area, and shots were fired. According to McCay, a newsman wrote about "the liveliest kind of war in south Jersey among the 3,000 oystermen."[99] More arguments ensued, and eventually the legislature authorized the New Jersey Oyster Commission to buy back the riparian grants.

In 1899, legislation known as the State Control Act provided for the issuing of a license to all persons engaged in the oyster business for a modest yearly fee. Grounds were leased solely for planting oysters. Bailey provides a long list of each of these leaseholders and of the boat licenses in her book *South Jersey's Oyster Industry*.[100] By 1903, the law also provided for the establishment of the State Bureau of Shell Fisheries.[101]

As present law now stands, all of the lands under the water belong to the state. Lands for oyster farming may be rented for a fee, depending on the location. The oysterman marks the boundary of the grounds by pushing stakes into the bottom. He applies to the Division of Shell Fisheries for a lease covering the area. As long as the planter pays the annual lease fee and his lease is approved each year, the ground is his for oyster farming. In return for rentals paid, the division employs watchmen who police the area to prevent theft of oysters.[102] (A list of oystering law in New Jersey is given in the appendix.)

The heavy shipping season is during October, November and December. Forty thousand acres of oyster beds were laid out by 1926, with seedlings then sown at a depth of ten to twenty feet. They grow there for three years before reaching market size. The natural oyster beds of the New Jersey portion of Delaware Bay stretch for about twenty-eight miles from Artificial Island at the upper end of the bay to Egg Island, approximately midway

Above: A busy day at the shipping sheds as men load large bags of oysters onto the boxcars at the right. The "suits" keep a tally. *Courtesy of Cumberland County Historical Society, photographer Harvey Porch.*

Left: Nicky Campbell, once an owner of the *Meerwald*, is shown with others marking off lease areas with saplings. *Bayshore Collection, gift of Ken Lore.*

down the bay, and cover approximately sixteen thousand acres. From upbay to downbay, oysters on these beds experience increasingly higher salinity that generally corresponds to a high rate of growth.[103]

Beginning in 1871, state statute required oystermen to have a license for each boat in order to transplant seed oysters from the New Jersey State Seed Beds (twenty thousand acres) to their leased oyster grounds in the Maurice Cove (thirty thousand acres). This occurred during the months of May and June, which were called "bay season." Traditionally, the harvest season occurred during the months with *r*s (September–April) when oysters planted three years earlier had grown to market size.

THE INTRODUCTION OF SHUCKING AND THE AFRICAN AMERICAN COMMUNITY

The first shucking houses were established at Bivalve in 1922, and shortly afterward, the McNaney Oyster Company shucking house was built in South Port Norris. Others followed, including the Phillips Seafood Packing Company, owned by Clyde A. Phillips. These modern oyster-shucking houses and clam-processing plants employed hundreds of people. Tonging of oysters, fishing, crabbing and farming offered other avenues of employment.

Shucking took place in the sheds along the wharves in Bivalve and in nearby Shellpile. Bivalve Packing Company, Blue Points and William Sharp were oyster-shucking houses run originally by operators from Maryland and then eventually by the local Robbins brothers. Sheds were heated by pot-bellied stoves. As many as seventy-five to eighty shuckers in a room stood at a station and shucked continuously all day, from 6:00 a.m. until at least 3:00 p.m. but sometimes until 5:00 or 6:00 p.m. or until the oysters were finished. Shuckers were originally paid by the gallon bucket but later by the pound. In some areas in the late 1800s to early twentieth century, workers were paid in brass or steel tokens provided by the shucking house. You got a token for each gallon, and at the end of the day, you turned the tokens in for cash. Locally, gallons shucked were kept on a tally board.

The practice of floating oysters in wooden cages to clean them and plump up the meat was banned in 1927 after an outbreak of typhoid fever was blamed on the floating of Delaware Bay oysters. The epidemic occurred in 1924–25 and was traced to Long Island oysters. The thinking was that floating of oysters near urban areas made them susceptible to picking up contaminants from the raw sewage in the rivers. Later, it was found that Delaware oysters were not responsible for any typhoid at all, but by then, the practice of shucking was firmly established and the United States Public Health Service had ordered the practice of floating permanently discontinued nationwide. Floating was replaced by washing the oysters in blowers resembling large washing machines and then shucking them prior to shipment.

In the mid-1920s, African American workers were recruited from the Chesapeake area to shuck—that is, remove oysters from their shell—and work as crew on the boats. They were at first seasonal workers who returned to Maryland when the season ended, but eventually, they and their families began to make the bayshore area home. The old oystermen talked about hiring the African Americans from places in Maryland like Crisfield, Shady Side (a small Black community near Annapolis) and Cambridge.

Georgia Robinson and others were interviewed in January 2009 by Bayshore volunteer Pat Moore. "All I remember is the breaking box and the bucket. There was a metal there, and you would hit the oyster on it." The most gallons shucked in one day was thirty-five. The shells went down one side of the box, and someone would come by with a wheelbarrow to cart off the shells. Once shucked, the oysters were dumped into a skimmer, and any juices were drained. The skimmer kept tally of each shucker's number of gallons. The oysters were then placed in a blower where they were washed. From there, the oysters went to another skimmer and finally were placed in cans. This process replaced the floating of oysters.

Shucking oysters can only be done by hand, and it is a tricky business. According to Shirley Bailey, "Workers stand on a wooden platform in individual stations with mounds of oysters in front of them. The oysters are opened by inserting a thick knife specially made for the purpose into the oyster and breaking the hold of the oyster and then moving the blade around to cut the powerful abductor muscle, loosening the meat. The meat is then dumped into one of three graded pots according to the size of the oyster. When a container is filled, it is taken to the packing room...weighed, and the shucker given credit for the pot."[104] Oystermen, whether shuckers or those on the boats, did not earn a great deal.

Clyde A. Phillips Sr., who would add the schooner *A.J. Meerwald* to his fleet of boats, would play an important role in the oyster business at Bivalve. In an interview on May 1, 2020, Clyde A. Phillips [Jr.] recounted that his dad became an oyster boat captain at the age of sixteen. Within a few years, he had married the boss's daughter from the Lake family, founders of Ocean City, New Jersey, and of Palisades Park in North Jersey. Leaving Maryland in the early 1920s, Phillips worked the boats into the 1940s.

When shipping oysters in the shell was banned in 1927, workers from the Chesapeake Bay area of Maryland and Virginia came to shuck the oysters. At first migratory, many eventually settled in the Maurice River area. *Courtesy of Cumberland County Historical Society, photographer Harvey Porch.*

An article in the *Courier News* of Bridgewater on September 11, 1941, names Clyde A. Phillips a member of the State Federation of Labor, representing the Oystermen's Union at Bivalve. In November of that same year, the *Courier Post* of Camden reported that mediation meetings were occurring due to a walkout by the Oystermen's Union. Operators offered 4.5 cents a pint or 36 cents per gallon to shuckers and a rate of 45 cents per hour to wheelers. The union countered with a demand for 38 cents for shuckers and 50 cents for wheelers. A total of 150 oystermen were out of work due to the closing of the shucking houses. Nine shucking houses, represented by William B. Stowman, were closed for the strike, representing nearly $100,000 in lost orders for the owners. The paper indicated one million bushels of oysters were harvested in one season in the Maurice River Cove, resulting in $2 million worth of business. In the end, on November 18, the *Morning Post* of Camden reported that Phillips could announce the shuckers would receive 36 cents per gallon compared with 31 cents for nine pints in the previous agreement.

Shuckers stood at their boxes, opened the oysters and then threw the shells on the floor and the oysters into pails. They were paid by the gallon. *Courtesy of Cumberland County Historical Society, photographer Harvey Porch.*

The following spring, the *Daily Journal* of Vineland reported on May 7 that seventy-five boats remained at their moorings as the boatmen asked for $30.00 per week as base pay. The previous year, they had received $22.50, and the company was currently offering $27.50.

Phillips built his shucking house in the 1940s and bought the *A.J. Meerwald* in 1947. The shucking house was located in the first section of the shipping sheds toward the Haskin Lab.

> *He tore down some of the sheds on his down riverside to create a firebreak. He had three docks and property up the river near the blacksmith shop. Built the shucking house out over the wharf, as was Hollinger's and Bivalve Packing. We handled close to one hundred shuckers. Two alleys for the wheelers—they wheel the oysters up to the shuckers from the boat. Shucking from September 1 or so, maybe Labor Day, the first of the season. Went until the market dropped—fell off right after New Year's Day. Week or*

two after. Used four or five boats in bay season but only one in the winter. Used the A.J. mostly, it was the best boat and held the most load. Brought in eight hundred bushels per day, but maybe not shucking all of those in one day. Over two hundred oysters per bushel, but [yielded] only one gallon of oysters shucked. They [the shuckers] were paid by the pint.[105]

Phillips died young at only fifty-two years of age on the eve before harvest season opened. He was $750,000 in debt due to a loan taken to expand his business. His demise was posted in the *Millville Daily* on August 30, 1957. He died in Port Norris. His obituary says he was "responsible for the strong union, comprised of packers and shucking house workers." Phillips operated the Phillips Seafood Packing Company of Bivalve with his sons. At the time of his death, Clyde Jr. was serving with the armed forces in Fussen, Germany, and son John was operating his father's boat in the oyster area.

After the union was formed, the time men and women had to work was cut and the amount of money earned increased. Freddie Smith, a packer, got eight dollars a day before the union and twelve dollars afterward.[106] But as Margaret Towner pointed out, "If you didn't pay the union you didn't work....If you didn't pay when you're supposed to they'd pull you off your box."[107]

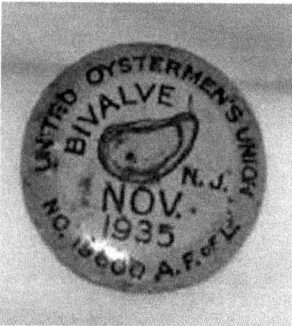

When the oyster workers were unionized, pay for the shuckers and wheelers increased. Clyde A. Phillips Sr. was the representative of the Oystermen's Union at Bivalve. A union button is shown, inscribed "United Oystermen's Union Bivalve N.J. Nov. 1935 No. 16600 A.F. of L." *Bayshore Collection, gift of Bill Biggs.*

The shucking houses were not quiet. In an oral history interview, Lionel Hickman recalled as a young boy, "When you would go into the shucking houses there would be a staccato-type noise of the breaking and opening of the oysters....Most of the shuckers had a rhythm, so it was not only a host of different sounds, but motion as well."[108]

Besides the noise of the oysters being broken apart, the shuckers often sang spirituals to help keep up morale and keep everyone going. "One of the greatest things was the prewar shucking houses....I loved it. I remember going down to the big house, Port Norris Oyster Company... down Shellpile....This was prewar because they would be singing the spirituals."[109]

Henry Hayes was a pro at the oyster business, working in shucking houses, serving as a crew member on the boats or harvesting salt hay in season. In an oral history interview for Michael Chiarappa, he tells us:

> *Of course, in them days a lot of them women could shuck oysters too. We had a lady down there named Clara Boston....That woman could shuck oysters and shuck them whole just like a picture. She didn't cut them up. When you open an oyster, you cut it out by the heart, but if you cut it back by the lip, that makes it bleed. If you got a whole oyster and it ain't cut up, just cut by the heart top and bottom, that oyster measures up in the bucket.*[110]

The shuckers needed a health certificate from the New Jersey Board of Health before they were allowed to work. The equipment used for washing and packing was inspected and licensed. Once washed and packed, oysters are pushed by paddle into the cans during the packing process and are not touched by human hands. Shuckers were invariably African Americans, while packers were white.[111]

Working on the boats was difficult work, and many of these men from Maryland were crew, and some in fact became captains. In an oral history interview in 2003, Robert Morgan mentions several: "Dr. Sharp's driver, John Cornish, he also was captain of the *Rosie Lambert*, which was a little schooner....Elwood McBride...he was a captain. Cecil Upsur was a boat captain. There were an awful lot of Blacks that were capable, but you know how things work....Things change slow." Chiarappa says, "The arrival of the African American oysterman in Port Norris...initially triggered a racist backlash in the closing years of the nineteenth century."[112]

The shuckers and their families lived in extremely poor conditions in company towns such as Shellpile and Berrytown. The town Shellpile was named for the huge piles of oyster shells, and of course, piles of shells create a pungent odor. The homes in these towns were of clapboard but often with holes in the walls that needed to be plugged up with whatever was handy. *New Jersey: A Guide to Its Present and Past* mentions Shellpile in a less than flattering light: "The shell roads are renewed each year as the mud swallows another layer of shell....The police stay out of their local fights."[113] A story is recounted that in February 1934, the boats were frozen in with no one in the oyster industry able to work and earn any money. A welfare society sent a truckload of food to Shellpile. Port Norris wasn't happy at being bypassed, and a second truck of food was stopped in the middle of Port Norris and distributed to white folk.

In an oral history interview, Beryl Whittington tells us, "It was a shame, it was a sin we had to live in them houses. There were holes....In the wintertime

Pictured here is the crew of the schooner *Mary Carolyn*: Captain Boyd M. Robbins (*seated*),
Captain Normand Robbins (*hand on pole*), First Mate Otis Davis (*standing right of Captain Boyd*).
The man with the apron is the cook, Buster Walker; the second mate, John Waters, is next
to the cook; the man in the back row, far left, is George Washington. *Bayshore Collection, gift of
the photographer, John C. Lore, 1941.*

we had to take boxes…and put up inside….I'm telling you how it was. I
don't need to tell you the good part. I tell you the bad part."[114]

At the time when Bivalve was the "Oyster Capital of the World," nearby
were "the barracks," rows of dwellings that lined a few narrow stretches of
road called Front, Back, Church and School Streets. The area was described
as "wooden barracks erected on stilts over the salt marshes. From 500 to
1000 Negroes here live their own lives in their own way and present a united
and rather hostile front to the rest of the world."[115]

At one point, there were perhaps 2,500 people living in the shantytowns.
Miller Berry owned two-story apartment houses of clapboard and rented
these out. This area became known as Berry Row. A social life evolved
with a small tavern where the men would gather, while the children played
games in the street.

These poor living conditions existed well into the twentieth century. An article
in the 1978 *Philadelphia Inquirer* talks about the consideration of public housing

The town was called Shellpile for an obvious reason. Shells were used to reseed the oyster beds to provide a hard surface for new oysters to grow on. *Library of Congress/Rothstein.*

A group of African American children, shown playing in front of the shipping sheds near the rail cars at Maurice River. *Bayshore Collection, gift of Olin McConnell.*

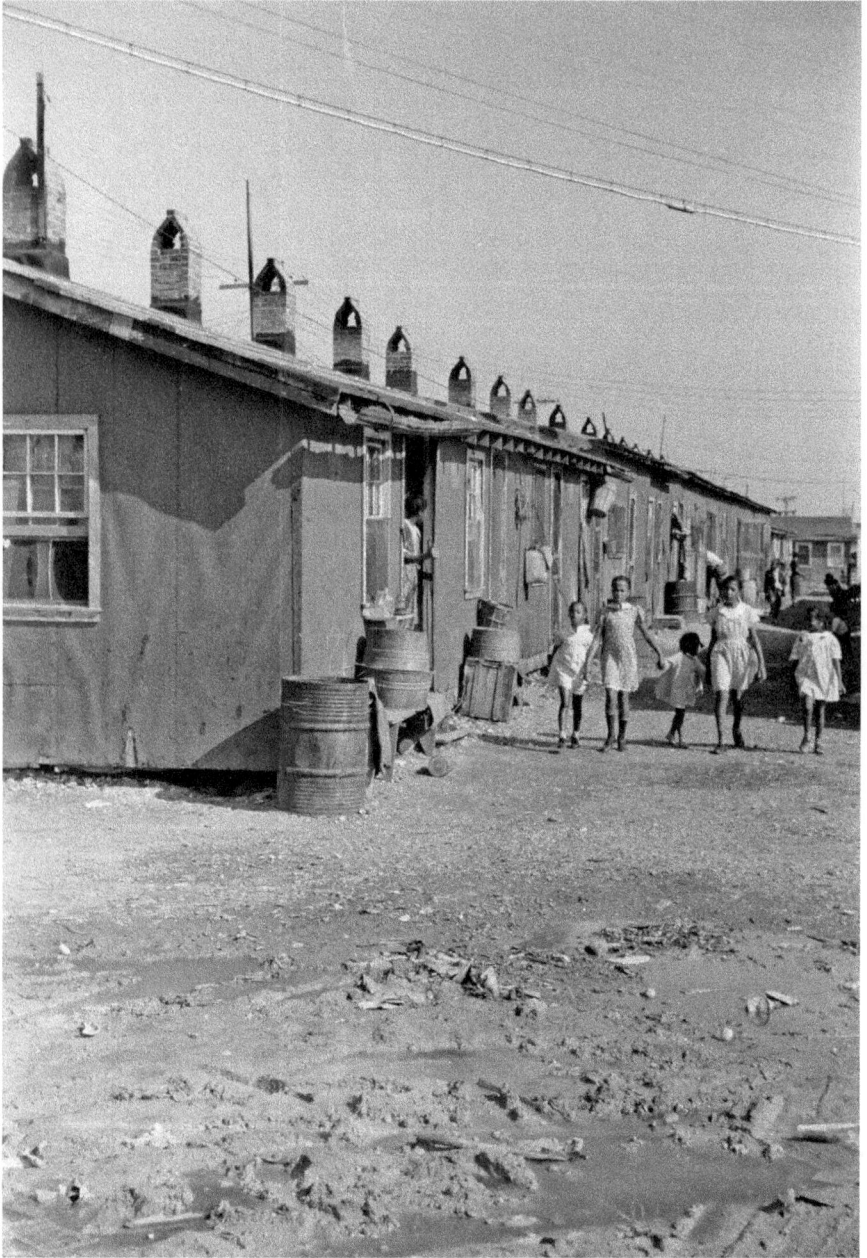

The town of Shellpile remained a collection of poor housing into the mid-twentieth century. *Library of Congress/Rothstein.*

to be built finally for those remaining in the area. "Mean little shacks built on hundreds of thousands of clam and oyster shells, shacks that contain no water, no toilets, no central heating, where crumbling walls are patched with rusted Coca-Cola signs, where rats scramble under floorboards and seagulls cry above the plastic bottles and moldering garbage that assault the reed grass."[116]

But here and in the other shantytowns, named Berrytown (after the family who owned it) and Frogtown (because its owner was called "Froggy" by his friends), the Black residents talked longingly of running water, of no more lugging pails one hundred yards from a shantytown well and of finally moving into the twentieth century.

"'The housing never was any good,' said Margaret Wise, who lived first in Shell Pile, then Berrytown, and now stays with her daughter in a decent house away from the shantytown until she can figure out where to go next. 'But I can remember in 1947 I could make $20 or $25 a week from September to April just shucking oysters,' she said."[117] She was fast, and $25 was good money in 1947, especially in those parts. That $25 in 1947 would compare to $291.74 in 2017, according to usinflationcalculator.com.

Berrytown realized a second claim to fame in the 1970s when CBS aired a docu-drama about the poverty of migrant workers and chose Port Norris as the location for the shoot. Using the backdrop of the shanties and run-down streets, Cloris Leachman, Ron Howard, Sissy Spacek, Cindy Williams and others treated locals to photos and autographs in the summer of 1973.[118]

"A lot of white people say that if blacks don't like it here they should move," said Dan O'Connor, a laboratory technician at Rutgers University's oyster research project. He said rehabilitation would be nice, but there wasn't any money available. He continued, "If they moved, the town would collapse. The oyster industry is coming back, and when it does, we'll need them even more than we do now." Unfortunately, O'Connor's prediction has not yet come true, though the shantytowns were demolished and residents moved to nearby public housing not long after the news article was published.[119]

Still, regardless of the poor reputation and conditions of Berrytown and Shellpile, there was a marked sense of community among the residents during the heyday of the industry, as seen in the following quotes from oral history participants DuBois, Ballard and Hickman:

> *I'd like to tell you the old crews we got from down there, they had homes, had their schools, they had their gardens, chicken, poultry, pigs; they were nice people. They'd come up here May and June and they'd go home and crab the rest of the season. The off-season for them was May and June.*[120]

We were poor, but we didn't know it. We didn't have anything....We had everything we needed. We didn't have everything we wanted, but we had everything we needed. We were just happy people.[121]

There was always music floating through the air...and very ruckus sounds that I still hear in my head.[122]

The next generation from Shellpile didn't go into the oyster industry. Ballard, for instance, became superintendent of schools for Commercial Township. At the height of the fishery, more than five hundred vessels (schooners and other types) and four thousand people worked in commercial oystering in Cumberland County. Many others were involved in processing, shipping, blacksmithing and other industries dependent on the oyster. Local folklore maintains that because of the oysters, there were more millionaires per square mile in Port Norris than anywhere else in New Jersey.

At the height of the industry, oyster boats lined the river and the docks. The schooners shown are "new style" or bald headed. Behind the sheds is a line of boxcars and, beyond that, the town of Bivalve. *Temple University Libraries, Urban Archives, courtesy of Michael J. Chiarappa.*

OYSTER RESEARCH AND THE DEMISE OF THE INDUSTRY

As early as 1888, research began on the health and nature of the oyster industry. Dr. Julius Nelson was appointed and conducted research on the boat *Ostrea*. Later, the Mott Station near Tuckerton continued the work, and by 1905, there were four stations at Bivalve, Tuckerton, Keyport and Barnegat. Eventually in 1923, a permanent station was built at Bivalve. In 1982, a new $1 million lab, the Haskin Laboratory, was established at Bivalve by Rutgers University.

The oyster industry began suffering from overfishing as well as a bad economy during the Great Depression. World War II and a shortage of manpower brought changes to the industry in the form of mechanization and the use of motors to replace sails in order to harvest oysters. The use of motors to propel the schooner hulls added safety and convenience, as well as efficiency of the workforce.

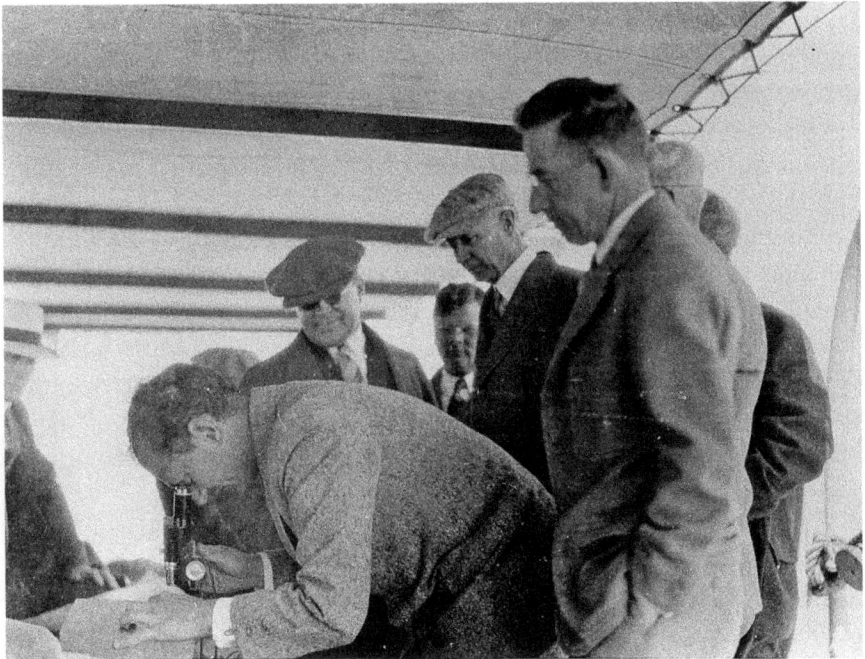

Dr. Thurlow C. Nelson, one of the early pioneers of Rutgers Haskin Shellfish Research Laboratory. *From Archives and Special Collections at Rutgers, New Brunswick.*

The Two Lessons

John McCabe wrote extensively on the web about the history of oysters on a now defunct site. McCabe suggested that there are two lessons about the oyster that man never seems to learn. The cultivation of oysters is the only way to ensure their survival if one must continually harvest oysters for sale. McCabe calls this "oyster lesson #1": oyster harvesting without oyster cultivation leads to no oysters being left to harvest.

Although this lesson seems to be self-evident, almost all the oystermen in all the countries of the world, and through many centuries, learned this lesson the hard way. Amazingly enough, some did not learn it at all and, in the first half of the twentieth century, went right on overharvesting what was left of the natural oyster beds, not only in southern New Jersey but also in other major oystering areas such as the Chesapeake, Long Island and Barnegat Bays.

In addition, in man's continued stupidity, the second lesson wasn't learned at first either. Since oysters grow well in estuary regions where rivers meet the sea, they grow close by where man's cities are growing, with the city having the tendency to pollute the waters around them through both industrial and human waste. Since oysters are natural filtering organisms, they keep on imbibing the waste, and as they are in turn eaten by us, the diners get sick and die—both the humans and the oysters.[123]

Once the Great Depression of 1929 hit, the Haskin Lab reports that 2.2 million bushels of oysters were brought in by the local industry, but by 1938, only 0.8 million oysters were harvested.

Then the major blow hit. In 1957, the Delaware Bay oyster industry collapsed when a mysterious protozoan (single-cell organism) known as MSX (multinucleated sphere unknown) started killing oysters. Within two years, catches had dropped by 90 to 95 percent. The disease, now also known as Delaware Bay disease, was introduced to the area by an unknown source, though some have speculated it was brought on the hulls of ships returning from the Pacific after World War II. Whatever its cause, the oyster industry on the Delaware was decimated.

The once thriving communities of Port Norris and Bivalve collapsed as the oysters disappeared. Some, like the town of Maurice River, located across the river from Bivalve, became ghost towns. The company towns of Shellpile and Berrytown were left to deteriorate further as many of the residents moved to find work.

Most of the shucking houses were unwilling to invest the kind of capital needed to convert to processing clams instead. In Commercial Township, only Riggins and Rawlings were willing to convert their facilities, but Riggins eventually sold the operation to Gorton's of Gloucester.[124]

Some oystering remained. After World War II, some help came when the use of power dredging became legal. Many of the sailboats were converted to power to make oystering more efficient, and by 1950, the Maurice River Cove was producing again, with some 900,000 bushels of oysters from over fifty thousand acres of oyster beds.[125] While this shows some recovery, the industry went from counting millions of bushels in the early days to thousands of bushels in more recent years.

But some of the oystermen had their own ideas as to what happened to the oysters. Mike Chiarappa quotes Beryl Whittington, a man with long experience shucking from Maryland to Port Norris:

> *That's what killed them* [oysters], *taking the sails* [off the schooners] *and put*[ting] *them motors on them great big dredges, that killed the oysters. Just broke them up, that carried them away…motorized dredging. As long as they had the sails they kept plenty of oysters. See, then they got greedy. They wouldn't clean the* [planted] *grounds in the spring-time like they did when I first come up here.…They stopped raking the grounds around I'd say '65.… That's when the oysters started fading away.…When they stopped cleaning them grounds, the oysters just wouldn't take and wouldn't grow.*[126]

The Haskin Lab was originally an agricultural station. According to Daphne Monroe of the Haskin Lab, Julius Nelson made the argument that the business of oystering was a type of aquaculture or farming. The station was first established by Nelson in 1880 to maintain the sustainability of the oyster fishing. The shellfish population is an important part of the ecosystem of the bay because the oysters filter up to fifty gallons of water each day, helping to keep the bay fresh and reducing pollution. It is also a very important piece of the economy in the area. Haskin's role now includes efforts on the part of the local ecology and working with the DEP and the fishermen themselves to set quotas and assess the stock.

MSX first came into the lower part of the bay by the Cape Shore in 1957. It was found first where the planting beds were. It had never been here before, so the first years had a high mortality rate of up to 50 percent in the seed beds and up to 90 percent at the market beds. "Hal Haskin started working on that right away. He developed a disease-resistant line of oysters by exposing oysters and leaving them for three years, taking the survivors and breeding them and then going back out and doing it again." While

MSX was significant in 1957, from 1969 to 1985, the presence of MSX and oyster mortality were low.[127]

It took time, but eventually, Haskin came up with thirty strains of disease-resistant oysters. Mother nature did the same experiment, and then thirty years later, in 1984 and '85, a massive drought brought less fresh water coming into the bay. MSX came farther up the bay and killed 90 percent of the oysters. The survivors were then naturally resistant to the MSX. It was survival of the fittest—they get it but don't die from it.

According to Monroe, the oyster population of the bay is still much lower than twenty years ago and one hundred years ago. The primary reason is a disease called Dermo, a single-cell parasite that reappeared in 1990. Scientists originally thought it was a fungus, but the parasite is sucked into the oyster and invades its tissues. The likely source was through seed oysters taken from the James River in Virginia. Like MSX, Dermo thrives in warmer, saltier waters, but it does exist in cooler water with lower salinity. This disease may have originated somewhere in the Gulf of Mexico.

Both problems continue to plague the oyster industry, but Rutgers University Haskin Shellfish Research Lab in Bivalve continues extensive research and, with the Shellfish Council, management techniques.

Ours is one of the better-managed fisheries and one of the longest managed fisheries. In the Maurice River Cove, the industry comes to the table, which includes the DEP and the oystermen themselves in a ground-up management style. Thus, the area still boasts a healthy and active fishery. Fishing rates are kept low and consistent, and beds in different areas are given different quotas depending on how the growth rate has been for the particular area. In-depth information on how the oyster beds are managed and how they are surveyed and assessed for their health and abundance is available in the reports from the Haskin Institute.[128]

There are different techniques used to raise oysters. New Jersey's oyster farms range along the sand flats of the Delaware Bay, where the waters include both the estuarine and ocean water, giving them a good mix of salt and sweet flavors. They are raised in mesh bags on racks just above the bay bottom.

The Haskin Laboratory works today to continue looking for ways to control MSX and Dermo, as well as to provide information on the importance of the oyster in our ecosystem. Clyde A. Phillips [Jr.] worked for the Haskin Laboratory doing oyster research as captain of its research vessel. "We went out every ten days and counted the dredged oysters and the spat. Thirteen to fifteen bushels of samples were collected on a daily basis. We would have two of us getting up to thirteen samples a day. They would keep us busy for two weeks, and we only went out every ten days." Later, they would use an oyster boat with a crew on board instead. "Inside of a week, we had all of it collected and most of it counted with four or five men on each side of the deck and two on the dredges."

According to Phillips, the Shell Bank program collected forty years' worth of information on water temperatures, tidal information and plankton counts in the Delaware Bay area. "We had forty years or so of constant data. Dr. Haskin and Dr. Ford went to these meetings around the country universities, and marine biologists looked at Rutgers with awe because we had so much data."[129]

Now, the Dockside Monitoring Program conducted by Rutgers is used to assess size and numbers of oysters per bushel. More statistics are taken yearly by Haskin during a direct market harvest. Twenty vessels were available for the process in 2019, a sharp decline since 2009, when seventy-four boats were harvesting oysters. This is attributed to a change in licensing that allows a single boat to harvest multiple quotas or licenses. The harvest for 2019 was 109,108 bushels of oysters, with the previous four years all reaping at least 100,000 bushels.

Much as it is satisfying to see the oyster industry stabilize after so many serious problems, a quick recap tells us that at its height, the Delaware Bay reaped 3,600,000 bushels, with over five hundred vessels plying the waters for that purpose. By 1950, the harvest was 900,000 bushels, still a much more substantial industry than we have now. In the early part of the twenty-first century, numbers reached an all-time low with as few as 20,000 bushels harvested, but by 2017, recovery efforts brought that number to 120,000 bushels. As of 2019, there are about eighty-three oyster licenses registered, while only perhaps a dozen boats are active.

Enhancement efforts continue. In 2019, over 160,000 bushels of clamshell were placed in the bed areas to assist in improving oyster density. Using the introduced shells to provide areas for the spat or young oysters to grow has been shown to increase density by an average of twenty-five oysters per square meter. Programs to continue monitoring and improving oyster growth are conducted not only by the Haskin Lab but also in conjunction with the Oyster Industry Shellfish Council and the New Jersey Department of Environmental Protection. Rutgers also produces oyster "seed" for the industry. These are future oysters still so small that they would have trouble surviving on their own. In Bivalve, Cape May Salt Oyster Company operates a dockside

Students from the UrbanPromise Academy in Camden, New Jersey, help on an oyster farm on the flats of the lower Delaware Bay with the program Project PORTS of Rutgers University. *Courtesy of Rutgers Haskin Shellfish Research Laboratory.*

building known as FLUPSY (short for "floating upweller system"). The tiny future oysters are given nutrients in a flowing bath of water until they reach half an inch after about six weeks. Then they can become bagged and moved to aquaculture racks or deep-water cages, where they continue to grow to market size.

Today, Haskin's Project PORTS (Promoting Oyster Restoration Through Schools) gives local kindergarten through twelfth-grade students and community volunteers a chance to participate hands-on in restoring the oyster habitat. Shell bags are constructed with clamshells and then taken out to the reef to serve as a surface for the spat to settle and grow.

Another program, with the Cape May Technical School, conducts a two-week aquaculture class where students can experience setting out systems to cultivate oysters and clams. Activities include installing racks, transferring shellfish stock and collecting data on juvenile and adult oyster stock. Students are even paid while gaining experience and interest in the shellfish industry.

Edible New Jersey lists over two dozen varieties of New Jersey oysters, principally from the Barnegat and Delaware Bays. Steve Fleetwood of Bivalve Packing describes the Delaware Bay oyster as "the perfect oyster. Plump, white meat, with the right amount of salt and a beautiful shell." The volume of oysters may not be what it once was, but the industry is not defunct, with Jersey oysters available from such diverse sources as the famous Grand Central Oyster Bar in New York City, the Oyster House in Philadelphia and the Oyster Cracker Café in Bivalve.

So, while Haskin, the Bayshore Center and other community groups work to maintain what is left of the once-thriving industry, there is light at the end of the estuary. The history is being preserved, and young people are being encouraged to get involved. While Dan O'Connor's optimism on the fate of the oysters has not entirely come true, a shellfish industry still anchors the Maurice River Cove.

Chapter 5

THE BAYSHORE CENTER
AND THE *MEERWALD* TODAY

SAIL…EXPERIENCE…SHARE…CELEBRATE
The Bayshore Center at Bivalve is a non-profit organization whose mission
is to advance the understanding of the human impact on New Jersey's aquatic
environment through education, advocacy, and programming. BCB operates the
authentically restored 1928 oyster schooner A.J. MEERWALD, New Jersey's
official Tall Ship, as a hands-on sailing classroom throughout the region. It
also operates the Delaware Bay Museum and offers shore-based programs at
its campus and schooner's home port of Bivalve on the scenic Maurice River in
Cumberland County.
—Bayshore Center website

*H*aving restored the ship and its home port, the shipping sheds at Bivalve, the Bayshore Center nonprofit began to take on a cohesive and exciting role not only in Cumberland County's unique wetlands habitat but throughout the state of New Jersey. Within the space of roughly fifteen years, the leaking sheds and sagging docks had been repaired and painted, full-time employees had been hired and the center had taken on the mantle of a protector of all things bright and beautiful about the community—the ships, the oyster industry and the all-important environment. The education mission has expanded, both shipboard and shore based, beyond the home county, and cultural, social and historic topics provide a much-needed sense of community down on the docks.

WHY IS THE BAYSHORE AREA SO IMPORTANT?

While New Jersey is best known for its Atlantic coast, there are fifty-two miles of bayshore along the western coast stretching from Salem, through Cumberland and into Cape May County. Cumberland County had been a busy, active place during the heyday of the oyster industry, but it is now a quiet area of old villages and many acres of crucial environment known as the salt marsh wetlands.

What is a wetlands? It is an ecosystem that is largely covered by water or has much water near the surface of the soil, perhaps seasonally, but especially during the growing season. Once, we called these areas "swamps." Now we know they are an important nursery for many types of aquatic plants and animals that thrive in the mixture of fresh and salt waters. Large numbers of birds are found there year round, but they are noted especially for the migration of species that rely on the wetlands as a stopping-off point on their lengthy journeys from North to South America and as far as the Arctic. The red knot is one such, staying on the bayshore for about ten days each year. And of course, the wetlands are an important egg-laying region for the horseshoe crab. Its eggs are crucial as food for some species, but also, this ancient species is crucial to scientists, who use its bacteria-free serum in the laboratory.

Over three hundred species of birds are counted each year, including waterfowl and wading birds. There are large, undisturbed stretches of coastline along the Delaware Bay. Consequently, the area sports the largest concentration of bald eagles in New Jersey.[130]

The wetlands also filter water to clean it of our wastes, chemical and other, and allow space for storm surges to spread without flooding coastal communities. On the Atlantic coast, we have carelessly built our vacation homes right along the dunes, filled in the marshes in many areas and created towns and cities in places nature never intended them to be. On our western coast, not so much. In the late 1800s, fashionable hotels dotted the bayshore. Steamships brought tourists from Philadelphia to take in the air and enjoy outdoor recreational pursuits such as fishing, hunting, excursions on the oyster schooners and boating. Over the years, the steamships went and the hotels were replaced with cottages. While there are isolated villages and small communities, they have never been large enough to do irreversible harm to the environment. Lately, especially since the impact of climate change, even those few homes in areas such as Gandy's Beach and Money Island are being bought up by the state government's Blue Acres program to prevent

The horseshoe crab is an ancient creature prolific along the bayshore. Its eggs are crucial to migrating birds as food and to medical science, which uses its serum. The crab is a favorite among children on education sails. *Wikicommons/Rhodendrite.*

further human invasion of what is clearly meant to be an animal habitat. Some villages such as Moore's Beach, Thompson's Beach and Sea Breeze have already disappeared. The Maurice River itself was designated a "Wild and Scenic River" by President Clinton. Area bumper stickers proudly call "No Retreat—Save the Bayshore."

"As the outboard engine was shut off, the only sounds were the wind rustling the phragmites on land, and the water gently lapping against the shoreline."[131] In a November 2017 article for NJ.com, Bill Gallo Jr. and Tim Hawk describe the peace and quiet of the remote cabins built for fishing and hunting in some parts of the wetlands. Generations of locals have owned these unlocked rustic shelters for years, located as much as five miles into the marsh. They are a local tradition. But the cabins are without a source of fresh water, power or sanitation, and the state DEP has declared they need to be razed once they are no longer repairable. The cabins are loved by their owners largely because of the isolation and the bit of pure nature they represent, but if the wetlands are to be protected, building is not an option.

There are some pockets of industry along Cumberland's coast, such as the remaining oyster industry, the clamming industry, marinas, ship repair and fisheries. One way of making a living in the wetlands area was farming. Areas along the shoreline were once diked to be farmed. Ken Camp owns one of two farms his father worked before him. And in addition to farming, Camp arranged rail bird outings and hunting parties. Rail birds are hunted from a boat poled through the marsh. Ken's father, Heis Camp, had clients who were wealthy men, including heads of state. Teddy Roosevelt came twice to Cumberland County to hunt rail birds. Ken Camp continued the tours into recent years. "You're out there in the morning, when the sun's coming up. It's the break of day. There's no noise. It is a pretty thing out there," Camp said in an interview.[132]

But restoration projects intended to preserve the wetlands outnumber industry. Some groups active in the area include the Conserve Wildlife Foundation, the American Littoral Society, the DEP and Public Service E&G, which operates nuclear plants in the area and has contributed to wetlands restoration at Thompson's Beach and Bivalve. Volunteers assist each year in the Return the Favor program, wandering along the bay beaches, turning over stranded horseshoe crabs and keeping a log of their efforts. The DEP Green Acres program in 2020 purchased wetlands along the Delaware Bay in Cumberland County to protect the habitat of waterfowl and other wildlife. A total of 204 acres of bay wetlands will be added to the present Heislerville Wildlife Management Area, which currently protects 7,231 acres of shoreland and the adjacent wetlands.[133]

The Bayshore Center, located on the waterfront at Bivalve, New Jersey, is dedicated to showing visitors the natural beauty of the Maurice River, including osprey and bald eagles, as well as oystermen and clammers working the river and bay. The center's mission is to "further the understanding of the human impact on the environment," according to its website. It educates the public in numerous ways, beginning with the popular sails on the schooner, the heart of the program.

Shipboard and Shore-Based Education

The *Meerwald* is the main artifact of the Bayshore Center and the icon of not just the bayshore area but all of New Jersey as well. When John Gandy and Meghan Wren first began the 501(c)(3), their intent was to prepare an educational program aboard the ship that would help people understand the importance of the oyster industry, the schooners and the wetlands ecosystem. Once the ship was restored, a captain and crew were rounded up, and the educational sails began. Now, from April to June of each year, and again from September to mid-October, groups of schoolchildren from grades four through twelve come on board for a three-hour sail. They learn the ship's history, hoist the sails, pull in the trawl net and learn about oysters and wetlands. Educational topics are taught by the well-trained and personable crew. While the captain and mate are generally a bit older and have to have the needed coast guard papers, the deckhands are often college students or recent college graduates. They come from all over the country, some on their first boat, but many having sailed anywhere from Maine to Florida or on the Great Lakes, often with similar educational programs. The most common college degree they share is in marine biology.

Allison Place is the former education director for the Bayshore Center. She says:

Like most people at a small nonprofit, I have worn a lot of different hats here based on what the organization needed at the time. I started on the crew of the A.J. Meerwald *as a deckhand/educator after I left another job to pursue a more meaningful career path. I had studied marine science in college and was looking for an opportunity to use my knowledge and skills to spread a deeper appreciation of marine life to others, specifically to younger generations. The A.J.* Meerwald *was a perfect fit. I fell in love with the ship, the culture and the looks of wonder on the kids' faces when they raised the sails or saw a horseshoe crab for the first time. After the season ended, I went to another boat, then a land-based job and then was called by the higher-ups at the Bayshore Center to fill an on-shore educator position here. I worked on planning, developing and implementing programs, as well as doing a lot of the operations work for the A.J.* Meerwald, *such as port permits, coast guard programs, crew hiring, etc. During COVID, we lost all of our school programs, and we had to think of ways to remain relevant in a digital world. We implemented our virtual education series, and we started opening up our programs to families and individuals instead of just to schools. These free programs have been widely successful and make the Delaware Bay accessible to everyone.*

The things that we teach here are so important. Kids do not get much hands-on learning in school, especially with digital learning. A day on the boat is worth so much more than a day in the classroom. Lessons learned by getting outside and experiencing the natural world will stay with the kids forever, and kids are freer to explore in ways that interest them. It's always surprising to me that many local children don't know that they live right near the Delaware Bay. Giving them the opportunity to not just learn, but experience, the beauty in their own backyards makes all the hard work worth it for me. I hope that we can continue developing relevant programs and bringing as many kids as possible out to experience the Delaware Bayshore.[134]

Most students coming aboard have a favorite education station: the trawl. The catch might include a horseshoe crab, some hogchokers (a small fish once fed to hogs), some shrimp or perhaps a small seabass. Almost always there are the blue crabs the area is noted for. Even in the chill of April or October, no one is anxious to return to the dock.

Dear Bayshore Center, Thank you for a very awesome field trip. My favorite part of the day was when we get to touch some fishes and crab and get to be in a boat but we didn't went nowhere in a boat. Your friend, Ashli.[135]

On weekends and in the summer, the *Meerwald* offers sails to the public in general, often with a theme, such as the pirate sail or a raptor sail. Summer also has some educational sails with boys' and girls' clubs or camp groups. Ports of call range along the Atlantic coast from Atlantic Highlands to Cape May and along the Delaware Bay and River as far as Burlington and occasionally Trenton. The ship can also be chartered for private or corporate events.

The *A.J.* is not just known locally; she is also a well-known feature along the Atlantic coast. For some years, the boat has participated in the Baltimore Parade of Sail and in the Chesapeake Bay Schooner Race each fall. She sails on occasion to neighboring Delaware to participate in the water festival at Lewes and has been part of Tall Ship Parades of Sail in Philadelphia and elsewhere. And the *Meerwald* and her mission have an impact on those who work on her. Monica Halverson and Charlie Cook were from the Midwest but came out to New Jersey to work as education coordinator and captain, respectively, on the ship. Monica Halverson reflects:

It was fate that took us to the schooner A.J. *Meerwald in the spring of 2004. We were recently certified as deckhands for square-rigged sailing ships as part of a midlife career correction. We were looking for our first professional sailing positions. As a middle-age married couple,*

The Bayshore Center and the Meerwald *Today*

The *Meerwald* participated in many years of Baltimore's extensive fall Parade of Sail, a gathering of forty or more schooners at the Inner Harbor each fall just prior to the Chesapeake Bay Schooner Race. *Courtesy of C. McCart, photograph by Frank McCart.*

just newly trained, looking to work together aboard the same vessel, it was proving difficult. One of the vessels in our pool of possibilities was the A.J. Meerwald. She wasn't a square rigger. Her primary focus was environmental education with predominately youth, which we knew nothing about. We didn't have much of an environmental ethic, knew nothing about the subjects being taught onboard (e.g., marine life biology, water chemistry, wetlands ecology, etc.) and had no experience teaching kids. It would not have been our first choice. But we didn't have any better options, so we took the positions that they offered us for the 2004 sailing season.

After only a few weeks into that sailing season, we were hooked and embracing the mission of the organization. We became soberly aware of many disturbing environmental issues that we had been oblivious to. This enlightenment helped us realize that we did have an inherent appreciation for the environment that had been smothered by the influences of our previous life choices. The organization's education curriculum also helped us to understand our accountability (on some level) for most every one of the issues we were learning about. A passion developed within us. We wanted to help others, young and old alike, through that same broadening, self-awareness experience in hopes of having a meaningful impact on environmental stewardship.

That passion continues today, which is why we say that fate is what brought us to the A.J. Meerwald. That first year experience had a profound and lasting impact on how we chose to carry on. We continued to work aboard environmental educational sailing vessels (including a few more stints on the A.J. Meerwald herself) through 2015. We now are residing in the Midwest, where our stewardship focus is on agricultural production in addition to simple day-to-day living. We can definitely say that it was that 2014 experience aboard the A.J. Meerwald that put us on the path that we continue down today. We will be forever grateful for all that she, and the organization behind her, provided us.

One final thought. The 1928 Meerwald is a relic of a sailing era and a booming oyster industry. Preserving that history is significant. But even more impressive than that is how effective she is in building community yet today. Shipboard crews dedicate themselves to the vessel and its mission. Countless hours of year-round volunteer effort keep her afloat. Participants of shipboard educational programs take great pride in having that experience because of her stature. Crews, volunteers and participants alike have an ongoing sense of collaborative ownership, which creates common ground and brings them together. We are honored to be a part of that shipboard community, which will keep us coming back in some fashion or another.[136]

SHIPPING SHEDS

It is March 2007. An eclectic group of new volunteers, staffers and old hands is gathered at the shipping sheds for the first day of volunteer training for on-board sailors. It is raining. We group together in the largest room downstairs on rickety wooden folding chairs with coffee and some of Meghan's terrific pound cake to sustain us for what will be a long day.

Meghan starts up her PowerPoint. She's going to outline the five-year plan for us before we begin learning, literally, our lines.

It is raining, but not just outdoors. We shift our seats to escape the drips, and someone gets a pail or two for the worst spots. We're huddled in our coats because if there's any heat in here, it isn't enough to ward off the chill. These are very dilapidated structures.

On the screen, she puts up the artist's rendering of how the renovated sheds will look in five years' time. We look at each other and smile—no way she'll get all that done that quickly. But thanks to the New Jersey Historic

Trust and New Jersey Department of Transportation grants and 2009 American Recovery and Reinvestment Act, within four years, Bayshore has a new set of attached buildings.
—Connie McCart

Originally built by the Central Railroad of New Jersey, the sheds were specifically constructed for the oyster trade in 1904, and the current roof configuration was added in 1916. This row of wooden buildings is attached to the wharves that line the Maurice River at Bivalve, docks where hundreds of oyster boats once moored. Now they are home to a handful and just one under sail—the *A.J. Meerwald.*

There are seven sheds owned by the Bayshore Center. The sheds were a way to efficiently move oysters from the water to the rail cars. They are fronted by the water, and at their rear, the railroad tracks brought in the train cars. Alleys between sheds line up exactly to load the oysters onto the freight cars. The sheds contained an office and storeroom, and other businesses related to the industry included a chandlery, a meat market, a post office

and a sail maker. The oystermen offloaded from the schooners into "floats," where they were left for a day or two to fatten, clean themselves and retain water and then forked into flat-bottomed boats called scows, which moved them under the covered wharves. There they were counted in bushel baskets, placed in sacks or barrels and then loaded into the boxcars on the other side of the shed.

One shed was purchased as early as 1995; the others came on board in 2001, and by 2011, they had been restored to their 1920s appearance. The signs on the sheds reflect their original owners— Hettinger Engine, L. Bradford & Sons, Berry Meat Market and so on. Inside the buildings now house museum exhibits on the oyster industry and the *Meerwald* and the offices of the Bayshore Center and program space. A separate gift shop building has recently been added.

The shipping sheds were originally built along the piers by the railroad company and housed many businesses complementing the oyster industry. They deteriorated severely over the years. Eventually, the sheds were restored to their original appearance. They now house the museum and offices of the Bayshore Center. *Bayshore Collection.*

On-shore education on the wetlands, oysters and the schooner mirrors the lessons on board the ship for groups unable to take the sail. Kids About the Bay is a land-based program that provides a

One on-shore activity for local students is the Kids About the Bay. Fifth graders from Cumberland County schools spend the day on the docks and sheds learning about the environment and history of the Delaware Bay. *Bayshore Collection, 2018.*

day on the docks to fifth-grade students from the surrounding, often low-budget, elementary schools. Other land-based education programs include Science on the Bayshore, the Bivalve Discovery Tour—which combines information on the shipping sheds and the heritage of oyster shucking—and the Wetlands Walk. School groups often combine these with a morning sail and afternoon on shore.

Today, Haskin's Project PORTS gives local kindergarten through twelfth-grade students and community volunteers a chance to participate hands-on in restoring the oyster habitat. Shell bags are constructed with clamshells and then taken out to the reef to serve as a surface for the spat to settle and grow.

Future plans involve expanding the shore-based programs to various ports, including programming specific to the Raritan River Watershed and Bay. Oyster bed enhancement will become part of the sailing repertoire, with passengers helping in the task of seeding the oyster beds in partnership with the Haskin Shellfish Lab and the Delaware Bay Shellfish Council. Overall, Bayshore's focus remains on teaching the importance of the watershed, the bay and the wetlands and helping its audience understand the human impact on this environment.

THE COMMUNITY

Dockside is the place to be. Especially on the second Friday evening of the month.

Since 2011, the Bayshore Center has opened its doors to the community for food, music and culture combined in a free evening of events. A raw bar on the dock serves up, of course, oysters and wine. Music might be a folk singer or Civil War–era band, or the audience might have to join in on sea chanties. The store is open for souvenirs, and a speaker is scheduled.

Topics feature a wide range; it could be poetry, gardening, history, climate change or the watershed. In a corner of Cumberland County where there aren't many events happening or venues open, the Bayshore Center has filled in as a place of importance to locals, as well as to the many fans and followers of the *Meerwald* from the tristate area. Recent events have included Oyster and Wine Tasting and Pairing; True Grit: Sandy Soil and Other Grains of Wisdom; Unkept Promises; Rising Tides: The Flow of Reality; and A Night of Revelry, featuring New Jersey poets, storytellers and musicians.

Looking for a day trip? The center also features the Delaware Bay Museum. The museum was started in 1995 with a grant from the New Jersey Historical Commission. It opened on Main Street in Port Norris with a collection of artifacts contributed by Al Huber, one of the original trustees. Now the museum is housed in the shipping sheds at Bivalve and has a part-time curator, as well as numerous volunteers. Archives have recently been reorganized, and oral history topics available to listen to online include such topics as Bivalve's history, the oyster industry, rope-making and speakeasies. Historic photographs can be accessed online as well. Exterior interpretive signage, funded in part by the New Jersey Historic Trust, allows visitors to self-tour the outer areas of the Bayshore Center.

Exhibits on topics tying into the water and wetlands are on display on a rotating basis, and permanent exhibits feature the oyster industry, from dredging to shucking. Interactive stations allow you to share in the oral history of the region. Volunteers and staff have compiled taped interviews with watermen, shuckers and local residents with a variety of backgrounds, including hunting and trapping, decoy carving and shipbuilding. Recent museum exhibits have included *Shipwreck!: Out of the Deep*, featuring artifacts salvaged by Atlantic divers, and *Skin & Bones: Tattoos in the Life of an American Sailor*, on loan from the Independence Seaport Museum, featuring artifacts from various local museums, as well as the museum's collection.

Visit the Delaware Bay Watermen's Memorial bell, and then take a walk on the mile-long boardwalk through the salt marshes and enjoy the wildlife and spectacular views.

VOLUNTEERING

Shipboard volunteers help with many aspects of sailing the ship, present programs to students and passengers, conduct dockside tours and more. The *Meerwald* sails from April through October. Volunteers need not live in southern New Jersey, as the *Meerwald* travels to ports throughout the state and region. Trainees as deckhands learn traditional boating skills, ship safety, regional history and the environmental and historical programs presented on board. No previous experience is needed, but volunteers must be at least eighteen years old.

Some volunteers come for one season and put in a few hours. Others stay for years. Tom Nichols is a longtime volunteer who has been with the Bayshore Center since 2005. He recalls:

> *Helen Jackson introduced me to the* Meerwald *in 2005. I went out on the first weekend sail in Burlington and took my dad. The next sail was from Riverside, where they were having some sort of festival. Mitch Brodkin was driving, and Bill was on bow watch and he called out, "Whale ahead!" Then he said, "Darn, I always wanted to say 'whale ho!'" It was fifty yards ahead of us, but we caught up with it. It was so close up against the boat that I could have stepped on his back. And so that was the trap that I got caught in. It was exciting.*

In his first year volunteering, Nichols accumulated over one thousand hours of service to the boat. "I kept going out on sails. I could sail from place to place. Riverside down to Philadelphia, for instance. I got so I wanted to be sure the boat was taken care of. It was 'my boat,' so I got my one-hundred-ton master license and sail endorsement so I could be a relief captain." By 2017, Nichols had accumulated over ten thousand volunteer hours on or for the *Meerwald*, five thousand hours in 2014 alone.

Besides sailing, Tom wound up with other areas of expertise. "Charlie Cook [the previous captain] got me into chart corrections. Each sail, we take a paper chart with us. Every week, the charts are updated by the coast guard. They make note of construction, of a buoy missing or one they've replaced, and my job is to make sure our charts are up to date."

Every winter, the old wooden boat needs extensive maintenance, and many volunteers work to put her back in shape for the spring. *Bayshore Collection, photograph by Seth Belmont, 2019.*

Those who aren't too sure about being out on the water can work on shore with the programs held in the shipping sheds or along the wetlands walk, volunteer on the museum committee, help out at Second Fridays, work on fundraising campaigns—whatever amount of time or whatever focus you might wish. You might become a docent, conducting guided tours of the museum, especially for student groups. Educators work either onboard the ship or on shore, sometimes with programs held at Bayshore, sometimes elsewhere in the southern counties.

And there are always those who volunteer specifically to work on the constant maintenance needed on a wooden ship. Again, this is an area where Nichols spends many hours. Besides yearly standard maintenance, the boat has been hauled out for major work in several recent winters. Nichols recalls, "I've worked on reconstruction twice—nine months one year where we reconstructed the mid-section, and then nine months in 2014–15 reconstructing the stern. We had to find material first, and then we stockpiled planks of white oak from North Carolina, South Carolina and Massachusetts. Jesse [Briggs, captain] was chasing white oak all up and down the Eastern Seaboard."[137]

The *Meerwald* tied up at Dennis Creek before being commissioned by the U.S. Coast Guard. The photograph was taken on a business trip by Lawrence T. Kessler from Pittsburgh, Pennsylvania, circa 1940. His son, Tom Kessler of California, found the photo in his mother's possessions after her death in 2019. Curious about the name, he Googled "A.J. Meerwald" and found the Bayshore Center. *Bayshore Collection, gift of Thomas Kessler.*

In September 2021, a second major restoration is planned to take place in Maine. In spite of the constant winter maintenance, a wooden boat is a needy thing. Recently, director Brian Keenan secured a capital grant from the New Jersey Historic Trust that will partially pay for another major haul-out to ensure the *Meerwald* can continue to sail. She'll sail north to Maine to be given the careful attention of shipwrights Tim Clark and Garett Eisele of Clark and Eisele Traditional Boatbuilding of Lincolnville, Maine. Clark and Eisele work specifically on historic ships, including the *Isaac H. Evans*, built in 1886 at Dorchester.

The *Meerwald* holds a special place in many people's hearts, especially those who grew up during the age of sail. In a note to the Bayshore Center, Joan Riggin Harper, born in 1924, writes:

> *While I am not connected to the* Meerwald—*I was fascinated when I learned a young woman, Meghan Wren, was determined to restore*

her to her former glory—so she could sail again! The boat was just as I remembered from my childhood. Later I became a volunteer. It was like going home for me; I was born and raised in Port Norris and all my family were involved at one time or another in the oyster business. Our boats were named the Tony Faust, *the* Addie S. Riggin, *the* J&E Riggin *and the* Timothy Bateman. *It is such a joy and a pleasure to see what Meghan accomplished and to see how the Bayshore Center is carrying on the legacy.* Joan Riggin Harper.[138]

The *A.J. Meerwald* continues to inspire the next generation of scientists, educators and advocates, as shared by Jenny Shinn:

As a Vineland native, I didn't have to travel far to find wild places to explore. As a child, I was drawn to the water; summers were spent fishing, crabbing and swimming. My parents instilled a love for nature in my siblings and I, and we all still enjoy spending our time on the water as a family today. When I was in the fourth grade, my family went on a sail aboard the A.J. Meerwald. *Our trip on the* A.J. Meerwald *was attributed to my parents' enthusiasm about the Delaware Bay. It was a memorable experience; there was so much to explore and learn at the Bayshore Discovery Project. I remember how exciting it was to help pull the ropes and maneuver the sails!*

Currently, I am a program coordinator at the Haskin Shellfish Research Laboratory, Rutgers University in Bivalve. The Haskin Lab is a world-renowned research center that has supported science-based management of the Delaware Bay oyster resource since the late 1800s. In this capacity, I assist with and lead research projects and community education programs. Unknowingly, I perhaps received my first lesson in oyster biology aboard the A.J. Meerwald, *and I now have the opportunity to share my shellfish knowledge with students of all ages at local schools during our programs. I enjoy sharing my love for the estuary and engaging the youngest of learners in local science. I still reflect on that sail, that experience and its influence on my career as a marine scientist.*[139]

CONCLUSION

In late August, a crowd gathers at Sunset Beach to watch the sun go down over the bay. The flag has been lowered, and Kate Smith has just finished singing "God Bless America." From upbay, an old-fashioned wooden sailing ship with all three sails full of the evening breeze makes its way down toward the pier next to the ferry slip. The setting sun is a huge red ball slowly sinking into the horizon, but nature pauses long enough at the water's edge to backlight the graceful schooner just as she sails between the concrete ship and the sun.

The crowd gives out a collective *aaah*, and the iPhones, Nikons and Leicas all click furiously to capture the moment. The *A.J. Meerwald* has become a symbol of all that is good about the Western Shore of southern New Jersey, the wetlands, the seafood industry and its watermen and the revitalization of a community once forgotten but now gaining back its dignity. And we're all moved by the romance of it all—men sailing under canvas, with only the wind at their backs.

Appendix I

OYSTER PRODUCTION CHART

*T*his chart shows the decline in the oyster industry in modern times. While millions of bushels were harvested between 1800 and 1929, with a high of 6 million per year between 1927 and 1929, the Depression caused a sharp decline by 1930, with a further drop of only 0.8 million bushels by 1938. In 1957, the disease MSX hit the area, causing a decline to only 10,000 bushels that year. In 1992, another disease, Dermo, attacked, and only 15,000 bushels were harvested. However, the business is alive and working. In 2015, 75,000 bushels were harvested, and since then, over 100,000 bushels have been harvested annually. Figures for this chart were available from Dave Bushek at the Haskin Lab.

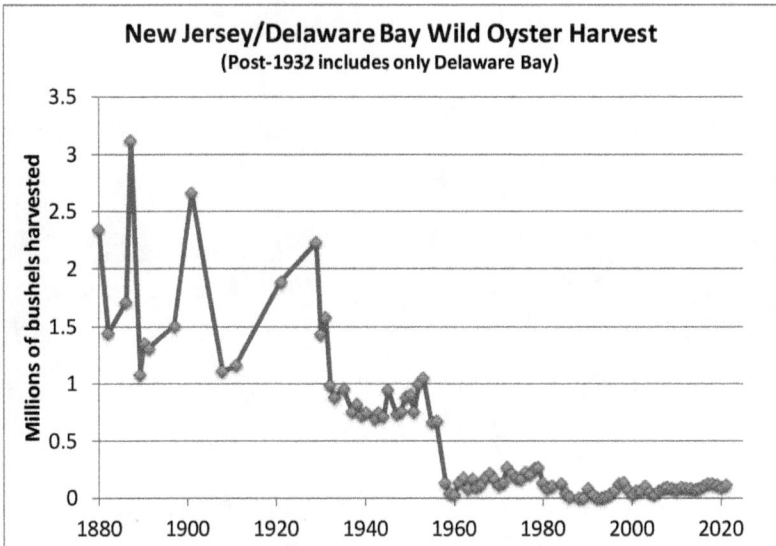

New Jersey/Delaware Bay Wild Oyster Harvest
(Post-1932 includes only Delaware Bay)

Appendix II

TIMELINE FOR THE *MEERWALD*

THE *A.J. MEERWALD* IN THE ROARING TWENTIES

1923–30: New-style oyster schooners, like the *A.J.M.*, are built to make improvements to schooner design.

1927: The Great Set: Spat (baby oysters) are plentiful and will ensure successful harvests the next several years.

1928: Brothers Augustus C. "Gus" and William "Bill" Meerwald contract with Charles H. Stowman & Sons Shipyard in Dorchester, New Jersey, to build the schooner *A.J. Meerwald* to secure their family's future. The boat is named after their father, Augustus Joseph Meerwald, a successful oysterman and a prominent member of the Board of Shellfisheries. Gus and his wife, Edna, use their home in Millville as collateral for the boat's construction.

August 31, 1928: The *A.J. Meerwald* is launched.

1928–31: The boat is used four and a half months per year and sells to shucking houses across the river from Bivalve in Maurice River, New Jersey, spending the off-season in Dennis Creek, New Jersey.

October 29, 1929: The stock market crash precipitates the Great Depression.

ENDURING THE GREAT DEPRESSION: 1930s

1932–39: Hard times fall. On July 23, 1935, the U.S. marshal sells the *Meerwald* at auction to repay creditors. The suit was instituted by Gus and Bill's younger brothers Francis and Edward. Gus and Bill's wives purchase the boat with backing from their parents.

1934: Gus and Edna lose their home in Millville. Edna's parents finance the purchase of a new home at the corner of Route 83 and Dennisville Road, South Dennis.

1935–43: The New Deal funds the planting of 8.2 million bushels of oysters. Programs build and improve fish hatcheries across the country, and New Deal funds are used for oyster drill control.

1936: Gus becomes a poultry farmer, joining his younger brothers. Bill is a justice of the peace.

1936–42: The *Meerwald* is inactive and tied up in Dennis Creek.

WARTIME MOBILIZATION: 1940s

1941: The United States enters World War II.

1942: The *Meerwald* is commandeered by the Maritime Commission under the Small Craft Requisition Authorization No. 115 of the War Shipping Administration. She is turned over to the U.S. Coast Guard and outfitted as a fireboat.

1942: According to Gladys Meerwald Brewer, Gus and Edna's daughter, the family put money into the *Meerwald* and were getting back on their feet, but the next four and a half years were marked by difficult compensation negotiations with the Maritime Commission.

1943: The U.S. Maritime Commission reports that the *"Meerwald* has the reputation of being one of the poorer vessels requisitioned."

1945: Delaware Bay schooners convert from sail to engine power for oystering.

January 1947: After nearly five years, the *Meerwald* is returned with $13,200 in compensation. Gus accepts the boat at Riverbank, New Jersey, but she is in poor condition, sufficient to make him cry.

August 1947: Edna and Florence sell the *Meerwald* and two oyster grounds to Clyde A. Phillips for $30,000. Mrs. Phillips changes the name to *Clyde A. Phillips*, and she operates under power, undergoing major alterations.

Appendix II

Environmental Reckonings: 1950s and 1960s

1957: The oyster industry is devastated by MSX, a protozoan parasite.

1958: The estate of Clyde A. Phillips is administered, and the boat becomes the possession of Harry Walton Sharp.

1959: Only forty-nine thousand bushels of oysters are sent to market, down from an annual harvest of one million bushels. Cornelius "Nicky" Campbell and Albert F. Mollinkopf purchase the boat and convert her to dredge clams offshore. Outfitting, including metal decking and hull sheathing, adds ten tons of extra weight.

1965: East Coast Trawling and Dock Company purchases the boat, amid a national environmental movement that pushes the creation of the EPA.

1969–85: MSX mortality is low, and oyster abundance improves.

Restoration, Resilience, Renewal: 1970s and 1980s

1977: Clyde A. Phillips Inc. (unrelated to the family) purchases the vessel, and the stern falls off while underway.

1979–83: The *Phillips* is idle. In 1983, the corporation merges with American Original Corp. of Maryland.

1983–86: The *Clyde A. Phillips* remains idle and is sold to the New Sea Rover.

1986: John Gandy finds the *Clyde A. Phillips* in Maryland and purchases her with the intention of restoring her to sail. Steve Carnahan and Bob Jackson bring the *Phillips* from Eastern Marine in Salisbury, Maryland, through the Chesapeake and Delaware Canal to Port Norris. It is a harrowing trip of sixty hours with many pumps working to keep her afloat.

1988: The Delaware Bay Schooner Project is formed by twenty-three-year-old Meghan Wren, who leads the organization for twenty-nine years. John Gandy donates the boat, the surf clam rig is removed and stabilization efforts begin.

1988: After ten years of being idle, the *Phillips* sinks in the Maurice River and is raised.

1989: Work continues at her mooring in the Maurice River.

NEW ERA AND RECOGNITION OF THE DELAWARE BAY: 1990s TO TODAY

1990: The pilot house is removed, and work continues to slow the deterioration of the boat. The Schooner Project is granted 501(c)(3) status, and Wren is hired as the executive director.

1992: The *Clyde A. Phillips* is lifted from the river and set on blocking in Bivalve. Work is achieved through volunteer labor, donated services and fundraisers.

1994: A full-time restoration crew is hired, working closely with a team of volunteers.

1995: The ship is rechristened as the *A.J. Meerwald.*

1996: The *Meerwald* is commissioned and begins a new life in environmental education.

1998: The *A.J. Meerwald* is designated New Jersey's Official Tall Ship.

NEW JERSEY OYSTER LAWS

1719: New Jersey Assembly passes the first law to protect the oyster beds from theft. Restrictions limit the number of vessels near the beds.

1846: It is state law that the oyster beds are closed during the summer months. This is the season when oysters spawn or reproduce. The Delaware Bay is excluded from statewide prohibition on dredges.

1860: Oyster cultivation—the transplanting of seed (baby) oysters from the state seed beds to oystermen's leased grounds—is common practice.

1871: A state statute is passed that requires a license for each vessel. Maurice River Cove and Delaware Bay Oyster Association has regulatory and law enforcement powers. Captains and owners hire a watch boat to patrol the oystermen's grounds.

1899: The Rough Cull Law requires that no more than 15 percent of empty shells be removed from beds. Spat (baby oysters) need a hard surface, preferably oysters or other shell, to latch onto and grow.

1899: The state takes control of the oyster industry. The Oyster Commission is established to provide supervision and enforcement. Later, this group becomes the Board of Shellfisheries and is currently the Shellfisheries Council.

1903: The Bureau of Shell Fisheries is established to handle leases and licenses.

1905: For dredging of seed oysters on beds, dates are modified from May 1 to June 30, what becomes known as bay season.

1905: Dredging under power is legalized on leased grounds.

1946: Seed beds are depleted. Planters co-sponsor with the Department of Conservation an act requiring that 60 percent of all shells be returned to the seed beds.

1959: Importing of seed oysters is banned. This practice first began in 1829.

1975: Year-round harvesting is begun to reduce MSX exposure.

1980: The seed fishery is closed to new vessels.

1995: Direct marketing of oysters from seed beds begins.

Appendix IV

MAPS OF NEW JERSEY'S
DELAWARE BAYSHORE REGION

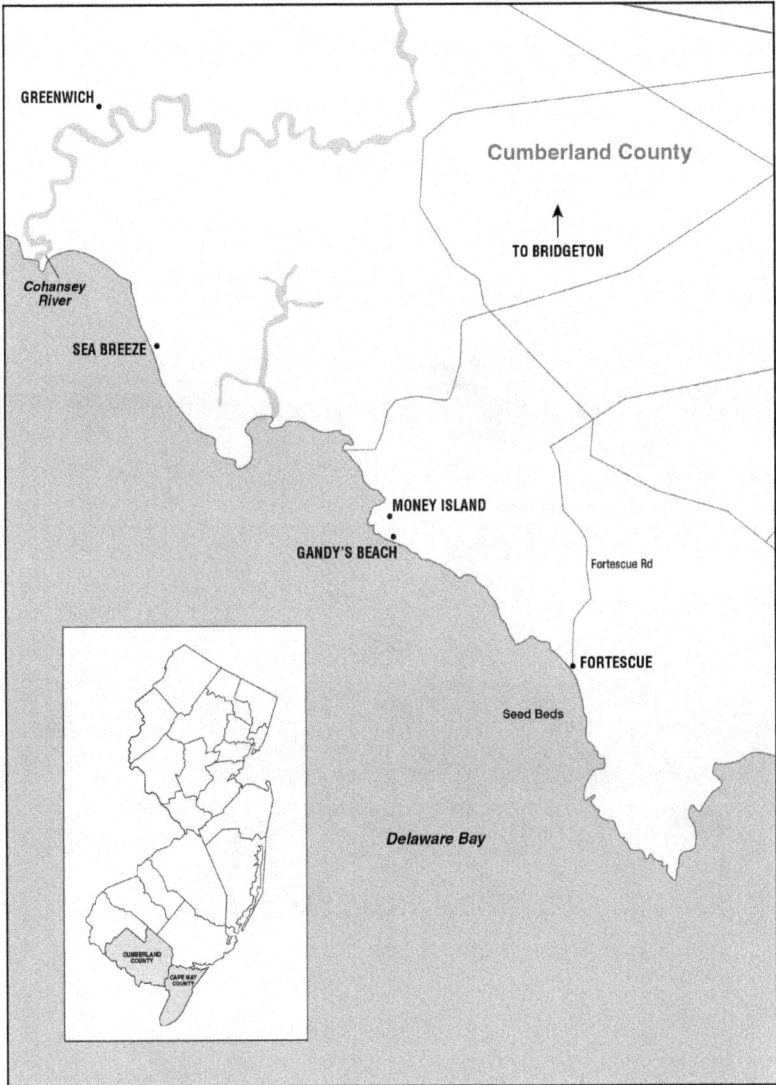

GREENWICH

Cumberland County

TO BRIDGETON

Cohansey
River

SEA BREEZE

MONEY ISLAND

GANDY'S BEACH

Fortescue Rd

FORTESCUE

Seed Beds

Delaware Bay

CUMBERLAND
COUNTY

CAPE MAY
COUNTY

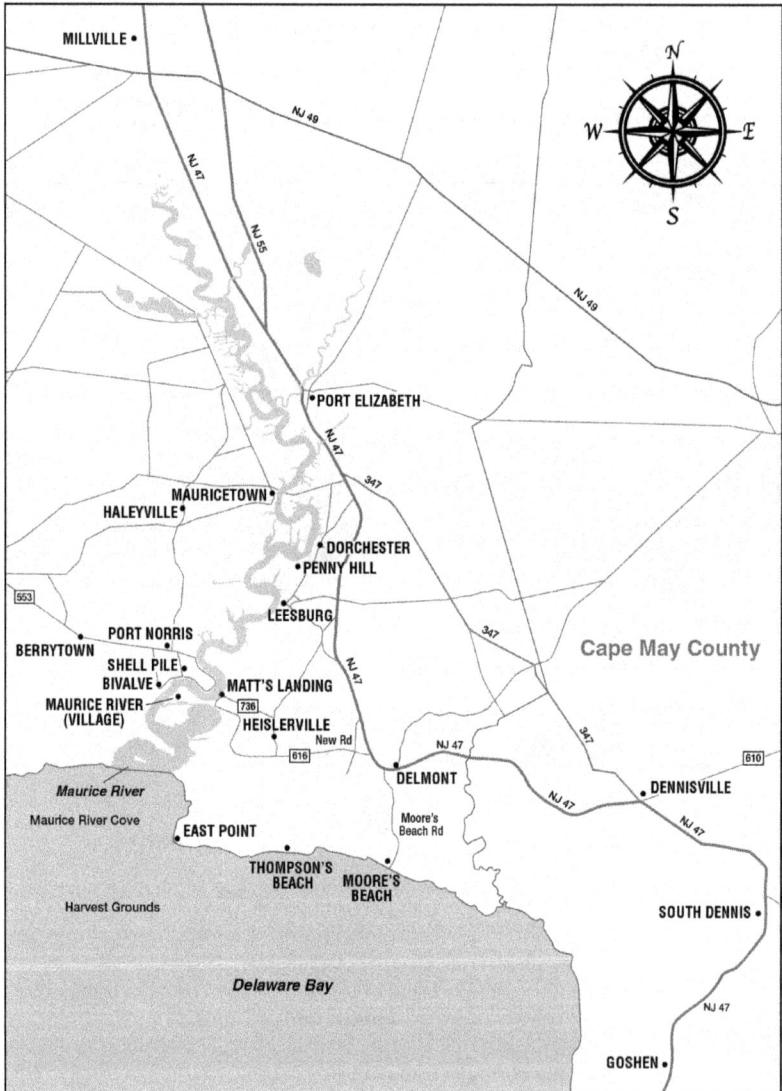

NOTES

Chapter 1

1. Rolfs, *Under Sail*, 40.
2. Cushing and Hiephard, *History of Gloucester.*
3. Tobin, "Meerwald Family Tree."
4. Canuso, "History of St. Elizabeth's."
5. Brewer, telephone interview, August 21, 2018.
6. Ibid.
7. Dolhanczyk, *Cashier Pilothouse* exhibit.
8. Wren, "Down Jersey."
9. *Vineland Daily Journal.*
10. Radu and Watson, "Oystering on the Delaware Bay."
11. Leagle, www.leagle.com/decision/194084537fsupp8081634.
12. Brewer, telephone interview.
13. United States Department of Transportation Maritime Administration Records (U.S. Maritime Commission and War Shipping Administration, 1932–50).
14. Bayshore Collection, funeral/prayer cards.
15. Phillips, oral history interview.
16. Daly, "Renewing a Heritage of Life on the River."
17. McDaniels, oral history interview.
18. Presti, *Schooners on the Bay.*

19. United States Coast Guard, "Merchant Vessels of the United States."
20. Lofft, "Restoration of the Oyster Schooner A.J. Meerwald."

Chapter 2

21. Rolfs, *Under Sail*, 10.
22. Joseph Conrad, *The Mirror of the Sea* (Rockville, MD: Wildside Press, 2003).
23. Koedel, *South Jersey Heritage*.
24. Lofft, "Restoration of the Oyster Schooner A.J. Meerwald."
25. Phillips, oral history interview.
26. Dorchester Shipyard.
27. Haley, *Schooner Era*.
28. Rolfs, *Under Sail*.
29. Witty, "'Cornshuckers' and 'Sandsnipes.'"
30. Cushing and Hiephard, *History of Gloucester*.
31. Witty, "'Cornshuckers' and 'Sandsnipes,'" 8.
32. Bickings, oral history interview.
33. Witty, "'Cornshuckers' and 'Sandsnipes,'" 64.
34. Ibid., 12.
35. Ibid., 33.
36. Moonsammy, *Smart Boats, Able Captains*.
37. Urgo, "When Oyster Boats Ruled Delaware Bay."
38. DuBois, oral history interview.
39. Moonsammy, *Smart Boats, Able Captains*.
40. Lore, oral history interview.
41. Moonsammy, *Smart Boats, Able Captains*.
42. Anderson, oral history interview.
43. Ibid.
44. Hickman, oral history interview.
45. DuBois, oral history interview.
46. Witty, "'Cornshuckers' and 'Sandsnipes.'"
47. Presti, *Schooners on the Bay*.
48. Ibid.
49. Moonsammy, *Smart Boats, Able Captains*, 126.
50. Presti, *Schooners on the Bay*.
51. Rolfs, *Under Sail*.

Chapter 3

52. McDaniels, oral history interview.
53. Wren, "Meghan's Story."
54. Wren, telephone interview.
55. Gandy and Gandy, oral history interview.
56. Ibid.
57. Schooner Project.
58. Daly, "Renewing a Heritage of Life on the River."
59. Wren, verbatim transcript of an interview.
60. Wren, telephone interview.
61. Pritchard, telephone interview.
62. Ibid.
63. Wren, telephone interview.
64. Edelman, interview.
65. Ibid.
66. Wren, telephone interview.
67. Benoit, email.
68. Gandy and Gandy, interview.
69. Ibid.
70. Wren, telephone interview.
71. Carroll, email interview.
72. Mitchell, "Clyde A. Phillips."
73. Wren, telephone interview.
74. Lofft, "Restoration of the Oyster Schooner A.J. Meerwald."
75. Wren, verbatim transcript of an interview.
76. Lofft, "Restoration of the Oyster Schooner A.J. Meerwald."
77. Cobb, letter to Martha Bark.
78. *Atlantic City Press*, C1.
79. Urgo, "When Oyster Boats Ruled Delaware Bay."
80. Wren, verbatim transcript of an interview.
81. Wren, "Meghan's Story."

Chapter 4

82. McCabe, oysters.us.
83. Ibid.
84. Bushek, "Can Oyster Reef Restoration."

85. Cushing and Hiephard, *History of Gloucester.*
86. Bailey, "South Jersey's Oyster Industry."
87. Buck, "Oyster Industry at Bivalve."
88. Baer, Coxey and Schopp, *Trail of the Blue Comet.*
89. Cushing and Hiephard, *History of Gloucester*, 245.
90. Bailey, "South Jersey's Oyster Industry," 13.
91. Federal Writers' Project, *New Jersey: A Guide.*
92. Bailey, "South Jersey's Oyster Industry."
93. Ibid.
94. Moonsammy, *Smart Boats, Able Captains.*
95. Hollinger, "Keeping Watch on the Times of Changes."
96. Ibid.
97. McCay, *Oyster Wars.*
98. Ibid.
99. Ibid.
100. Bailey, "South Jersey's Oyster Industry," 15–17.
101. Radu and Watson, "Oystering on the Delaware Bay."
102. McCay, *Oyster Wars.*
103. Buck, "Oyster Industry at Bivalve."
104. Bailey, "South Jersey's Oyster Industry."
105. Phillips, oral history interview.
106. Smith, oral history interview.
107. Towner, oral history interview.
108. Chiarappa, "Working the Delaware Estuary."
109. Phillips, oral history interview.
110. Chiarappa, "Working the Delaware Estuary."
111. Port Norris Historical Society.
112. Chiarappa, "Working the Delaware Estuary," 75.
113. Federal Writers' Project, *New Jersey: A Guide.*
114. Whittington, oral history interview.
115. Wren, "Down Jersey."
116. Severo, "Shell Pile, NJ."
117. Ibid.
118. Port Norris Historical Society.
119. Severo, "Shell Pile, NJ."
120. DuBois, oral history interview.
121. Ballard, oral history interview.
122. Hickman, oral history interview.
123. McCabe, oysters.us.

124. Hollinger, "Keeping Watch on the Times of Changes."
125. Radu and Watson, "Oystering on the Delaware Bay."
126. Chiarappa, "Working the Delaware Estuary," 82.
127. Monroe, oral history interview.
128. Morson, Bushek and Gius, "Stock Assessment Workshop."
129. Phillips, telephone interview.

Chapter 5

130. Natural Resources Conservation Service, "Wetlands."
131. Hillman, oral history interview.
132. Camp, oral history interview.
133. New Jersey Conference of Mayors, "NJ DEP Announces Purchase."
134. Place, interview.
135. Bayshore Center brochure, 2019.
136. Halverson, email discussion.
137. Nichols, telephone interview.
138. Harper, note.
139. Shinn, interview.

REFERENCES

Anderson, Fenton. Oral history interview by Mary Rita Zorn Moonsammy. Port Norris, NJ, March 18, 1988.

Atlantic City Press. "Whitman Sails Tall Ship." April 22, 1997.

Baer, Christopher T., William Coxey and Paul W. Schopp. *The Trail of the Blue Comet: A History of the Jersey Central's New Jersey Southern Division*. Palmyra, NJ: West Jersey Chapter of the National Railway Historical Society, 1994.

Bailey, Shirley R. "South Jersey's Oyster Industry." Yesteryear Series #5. *South Jersey Magazine*, Millville, NJ, 1999, 2–3, 7–12, 15–17.

Ballard, Barry. Oral history interview by William May. Port Norris, NJ, March 1, 2010.

Benoit, Suzanne. Email to Rachel Dolhanczyk, October 2, 2020.

Bickings, Harold. Oral history interview by Mary Rita Zorn Moonsammy. Port Norris, NJ, December 15, 1983.

Brewer, Gladys. Telephone interview by Rachel R. Dolhanczyk. August 21, 2018, and October 2, 2018.

Buck, G.H. "The Oyster Industry at Bivalve." *Reading Railroad Magazine*, January 1926.

Bushek, David. Quoted in "Can Oyster Reef Restoration across the US Impact What We Eat?" by Lela Nargi. salon.com, January 24, 2021.

Camden, New Jersey. "Oysters." www.dvrbs.com/camden/CamdenNJ-Oysters.htm.

Camp, Richard. Oral history interview by Rachel Dolhanczyk. "Voices from the Fisheries," July 18, 2013. voices.nmfs.noaa.gov/index.php/richard-camp.

Canuso, Helen Meerwald. "History of St. Elizabeth's Roman Catholic Church, Goshen, New Jersey." Self-published, n.d.

Cape May County Gazette. Obituary for A.J. Meerwald Sr. July 10, 1903, 3.

Carroll, Captain Tom. Email interview by Rachel Dolhanczyk. December 15, 2020.

Chiarappa, Michael J. Interview by Rachel R. Dolhanczyk. Bayshore Center at Bivalve, Bivalve, NJ, August 9, 2020.

———. "Working the Delaware Estuary: African American Cultural Landscapes and the Contours of Environmental Experience." *Buildings and Landscapes* 25, no. 1 (Spring 2018): 64–91.

Cobb, Jessica. Letter to Martha Bark, New Jersey assemblywoman, May 1997. Bayshore Center Archives.

Courier News (Bridgewater, NJ). "State Federation of Labor Elects Officers." September 11, 1941.

Courier Post (Camden, NJ). "Protesting Bill." April 4, 1940.

Cushing, Thomas, MD, and Charles E. Hiephard, Esq. *History of Gloucester, Salem and Cumberland Counties.* Philadelphia: J.P. Lippincott & Co., 1883, 914–18.

Daily Journal (Vineland, NJ). "Clyde Phillips Gets Labor's Nod." October 26, 1943.

Daly, Joe. "Renewing a Heritage of Life on the River." *Philadelphia Inquirer,* August 11, 1989.

Dolhanczyk, Rachel R. *Cashier Pilothouse* exhibit. Bayshore Center, 2016.

———. "A Timeline: The AJ Meerwald, 1920 to Present." Bayshore Center, Bivalve, NJ, 2018.

———. "Who Are the Meerwalds? 7 Generations from 1833 to Present." Slide show, Bayshore Center, Bivalve, NJ, 2018.

Dollar Weekly News (Vineland, NJ). "Fine New Sloop Ready for Water." August 21, 1928.

Dorchester Shipyard. www.dorchestershipyard.com.

DuBois, John. Oral history interview by Meghan Wren. "Oystermen Stories: Voices from the Fisheries." November 12, 1998. voices.nmfs.noaa.gov/oystermen-stories.

Edelman, Milt. Telephone interview by Rachel R. Dolhanczyk. April 30, 2020.

Edible New Jersey. "A Guide to New Jersey Oysters." High summer 2017. ediblejersey.ediblecommunities.com/search/content/nj%20oysters.

Federal Writers' Project of the Works Progress Administration for the State of New Jersey. *New Jersey: A Guide to Its Present and Past.* N.p., 1939, 639, 640.

Gandy, John, and Rona Gandy. Oral history interview by Rachel R. Dolhanczyk. Bayshore Center, Bivalve, NJ, November 1, 2019.

References

Haley, Neale. *The Schooner Era: A Lost Epic in History*. Cranbury, NJ: Barnes & Co., 1972, 116.

Halverson, Monica. Email discussion with C. McCart, January 2021.

Harper, Joan Riggin. Note to Rachel Dolhanczyk, March 2, 2021.

Heston, Alfred M. *South Jersey: A History, 1664–1924*. Vol. 3. Camden, NJ: Lewis Historical Publishing Company, 1924.

Hickman, Lionel. Oral history interview by Sally Van deWater. Bayshore Center, Bivalve, NJ, July 8, 2005.

Hillman, Jode. Oral history interview by Rachel Dolhanczyk. "Voices from the Fisheries." July 2, 2013. voices.nmfs.noaa.gov/index.php/jode-hillman.

Hollinger, Warrington. "Keeping Watch on the Times of Changes." Citizens United to Protect the Maurice River and Its Tributaries, Inc., 2002. www.cumauriceriver.org/downjersey/maritime.

Koedel, R. Craig. *South Jersey Heritage: A Social, Economic, and Cultural History*. Washington, D.C.: University Press of America, 1979, 115–24. westjersey.org/sjh/sjh_chap_10.htm.

Lofft, Charles. "Restoration of the Oyster Schooner A.J. Meerwald." Report for the Society of Naval Architects and Marine Engineers, Philadelphia Section. May 6, 1996.

Lore, Joe. Oral history interview by Meghan Wren. "Oystermen Stories: Voices from the Fisheries." November 12, 1998. voices.nmfs.noaa.gov/oystermen-stories.

Mauricetown Historical Society. mauricetownhistoricalsociety.org.

McCabe, John. "The Greeks" and "The Romans." 2005. oysters.us/primordial.html.

McCay, Bonnie J. *Oyster Wars and the Public Trust*. Tucson: University of Arizona Press, 1998, 22, 23, 24, 84–94, 117, 119.

McDaniels, Donnie. Oral history interview by Sally Van de Water and Deb Slating. "Voices from the Fisheries." September 12, 2007. voices.nmfs.noaa.gov.

———. Telephone interview by Rachel Dolhanczyk. September 18, 2020.

Millville Daily News. "Obituary, Clyde A. Phillips Sr." August 30, 1957.

Mitchell, Bob. "The Clyde A. Phillips aka AJ Meerwald." Newporter 40 Together, April 29, 2009. newporterworks.ning.com/forum/topics/the-clyde-a-phillips-aka-aj.

Monroe, Daphne. Oral history interview by Rachel R. Dolhanczyk. Bayshore Center, Bivalve, NJ, July 12, 2014.

REFERENCES

Moonsammy, Mary Rita Zorn. *Smart Boats, Able Captains: The Schooner as Metaphor in Port Norris, New Jersey*. Philadelphia: University of Pennsylvania, 2008, 94, 95.

Morgan, Robert. Oral history interview by Rachel R. Dolhanczyk. Bayshore Center, Bivalve, NJ, July 12, 2014.

Morning Post. "750 Oystermen End Strike for More Pay." November 18, 1941.

Morson, Jason, David Bushek and Jennifer Gius, eds. "Stock Assessment Workshop: New Jersey Delaware Bay Oyster Beds." Rutgers. February 11–12, 2020. hsrl.rutgers.edu/SAWreports/SAW2020.pdf.

Natural Resources Conservation Service of NJ, United States Department of Agriculture. "Wetlands." www.nrcs.usda.gov/wps/portal/nrcs/detail/nj/technical/ecoscience/bio/?cid=nrcs141p2_018658.

New Jersey Conference of Mayors. "NJ DEP Announces Purchase of Wetlands in Cumberland County." newjerseyconferenceofmayors.com/2021uncategorized/nj-dep-announces-purchase-of-wetlands-in-cumberland-county.

New Jersey Eastern Oyster Direct Market Landing Totals for Delaware Bay, 2006 to 2015. NJDEP, NJ Division of Fish and Wildlife, Bureau of Shellfisheries, 2016.

Nichols, Tom. Telephone interview by C. McCart. January 18, 2021.

Phillips, Clyde A., [Jr.]. Oral history interview by Patricia A. Moore. February 28, 2008. "Voices from the Fisheries." voices.nmfs.noaa.gov.

———. Telephone interview by Rachel R. Dolhanczyk. April 24, 2020, and May 1, 2020.

Place, Allison. Interview by C. McCart. February 2021.

Planning Documents. Submission for the grant from NJ Historic Trust, Bayshore Center, Bivalve, NJ.

Port Norris Historical Society. "Commercial Township, 1874–1974." historicportnorris.org/commercialtwp.htm.

Presti, Louis. *Schooners on the Bay*. Documentary. Dept. of State, NJ Historical Commission, 1984.

Pritchard, Charles. Telephone interview by Rachel R. Dolhanczyk. June 9, 2020.

Radu, Cristina, and Penelope S. Watson. "Oystering on the Delaware Bay." Annual Conference of the Vernacular Architecture Forum. Galloway, NJ, May 2014, 39–48.

Rolfs, D.H. *Under Sail: The Dredgeboats of Delaware Bay: A Pictorial and Maritime History*. Millville, NJ: Wheaton Historical Association, 1971.

References

Schooner Project. "Minutes" (logbook). Bayshore Center Archives, Bivalve, NJ, 1988.

Severo, Richard. "Shell Pile, NJ, Longs for a Comeback of Its Oyster Industry." *New York Times*, June 7, 1978.

Shinn, Jenny. Interview by Brian Keenan, 2020.

Smith, Freddie. Oral history interview by Patricia Moore and Olin McConnell. "Voices from the Fisheries." July 7, 2008. voices.nmfs.noaa.gov/freddie-smith.

Tobin, Edward. "Meerwald Family Tree." 2020. www.salinasramblersmc.org/tobin/Family_Tree/Meerwald.htm.

Towner, Margaret. Oral history interview by Meghan Wren. "Shuckers' Tales: Voices from the Fisheries." January 24, 2009. voices.nmfs.noaa.gov/index.php/shuckers-tales.

Tyler, D.B. *The Bay & River, Delaware: A Pictorial History*. Cambridge MD: Cornell Maritime Press, 1955.

United States Coast Guard. "Merchant Vessels of the United States." www.dco.uscg.mil/Our-Organization/Assistant-Commandant-for-Prevention-Policy-CG-5P/Inspections-Compliance-CG-5PC-/Office-of-Investigations-Casualty-Analysis/Merchant-Vessels-of-the-United-States.

United States Department of Agriculture. Natural Resources Conservation Service, New Jersey. "Wetlands." 1990. nrcs.usda.gov/wps/portal/nrcs/main/national/water/wetlands.

United States Department of Transportation. Maritime Administration Records. U.S. Maritime Commission and War Shipping Administration, 1932–50.

Urgo, Jacqueline L. "When Oyster Boats Ruled Delaware Bay and Port Norris Was N.J.'s Wealthiest Town." *Philadelphia Inquirer*, April 3, 2017.

Vineland Daily Journal. "Oysterman Loses Life in High Gale." May 7, 1929.

Whittington, Beryl. Oral history interview by Meghan Wren. "Shuckers' Tales: Voices from the Fisheries." January 24, 2009. voices.nmfs.noaa.gov/index.php/shuckers-tales.

Witty, Anne. "'Cornshuckers' and 'Sandsnipes': The Oystering Schooners of Delaware Bay." Thesis, University of Delaware, August 1984, 6.

Wren, Meghan. "Down Jersey: The Maritime Connection." Citizens United to Protect the Maurice River and Its Tributaries, Inc., 1999. www.cumauriceriver.org/downjersey/maritime.

———. "Meghan's Story." Appendix F1, Training Manual, March 15, 2013. Bayshore Center.

———. Oral history interview by Rachel R. Dolhanczyk. Bayshore Center, Bivalve, NJ, January 11, 2018.

———. Telephone interview by Rachel R. Dolhanczyk. April 15, 2020.

———. Verbatim transcript of an interview by Meghan Wren, executive director, the Delaware Bay Schooner Project, January 18, 1993. Traditional Small Craft Association, Philadelphia Maritime Museum Chapter.

ABOUT THE AUTHORS

onstance L. McCart, EdD, is a retired school administrator and teacher, a graduate of Rowan and Temple Universities. She resides in the Turnersville section of Washington Township with best buddy Winston, an English cocker. She enjoys spending time with family and friends and traveling. Dr. McCart has been a longtime member of the Washington Twp. Historic Preservation Commission and the Friends of the Heggan Library. A highlight of the eleven years spent as an onboard educator with the *A.J. Meerwald* was sailing in the Great Chesapeake Bay Schooner Race. Volunteering on the *A.J.* was the motivation for this book. Other publications include *Grenloch Terrace, the Most Beautiful Spot in South Jersey* (Instantpublisher.com, 2011); *From Beau's Kitchen* (Instantpublisher. com, 2010); Images of America: *Washington Township, Gloucester County* (Arcadia Publishing, 2009); *The ACES Project: Logan Township's Journey Toward Infusion of the Arts* (Logan Township School District and the NJ Council of the Arts, 2005); and *Prescriptions for Better Writing* (NJ State Department of Education, 1988).

achel Rodgers Dolhanczyk, MA, has been the museum curator at the Bayshore Center at Bivalve's Delaware Bay Museum since 2010. A native of the Berkshire Hills of Massachusetts, she found her way to the water and has worked in the history field for over twenty years along New Jersey's waterfronts and the Chesapeake Bay. Dolhanczyk is a graduate of Miss Hall's School in Pittsfield, Massachusetts, and has a BA in history from Wheaton College (Massachusetts) and an MA in museum education from the University of the Arts in Philadelphia. She spent a semester enrolled in the Williams College–Mystic Seaport Coastal and Ocean Studies Program. In 2004, she received an Award of Recognition from the New Jersey Historical Commission for her outstanding service to the public knowledge and preservation of New Jersey's history. She lives in a two-hundred-year-old house in Cape May County with her husband and children, who also enjoy all things history.

All proceeds from this book will go to the 2021–22 restoration and ongoing maintenance of the *A.J. Meerwald.*

Visit us at
www.historypress.com

www.ingramcontent.com/pod-product-compliance
Lightning Source LLC
Chambersburg PA
CBHW060318100426
42812CB00003B/812